Are you
Worthy?

Powerful steps for a resounding "YES"

Are you
Worthy?

Powerful steps for a resounding "YES"

MICHELLE HOLLINGER

Are You
Worthy?
Powerful steps for a resounding "YES"
Copyright 2019
Hollinger Publications, Inc.

ISBN: 9781098832339

Hollinger Publications, Inc.
Parlin, NJ 08859
www.hollingerpublications.com

Dedicated to

Gabrielle Union-Wade

PRAISE FOR "ARE YOU WORTHY?"

"Michelle Hollinger has not only claimed her worth; she has opened out a way for everyone to claim their worth, too. Her practical insights and examples awaken us from the 'illusion of unworthiness' to the reality that 'worthy' is who we are and shall ever be."

Rev. Dr. Sheila R. McKeithen,
President, Universal Foundation for Better Living
Senior Minister, The Universal Centre of Truth in Kingston, Jamaica
Author, 12 Steps to Healing

"'TOUCH DOWN," "HOMERUN," "4 POINT PLAY"!!!!! This book is empowering, well-written and super easy to relate to and understand. It could be the piece which is the nexus between "seekers" and New Thought. We are what many people are looking for. Thank you for saying "Yes" to being the channel through which this message is shared."

Rev. Dr. Anna Price
Provost and Academic Dean
Johnnie Colemon Theological Seminary
Miami Gardens, FL

"If you have embarked upon your healing journey and feel it can be a lonely and sometimes, painful road, I implore you to let the words from Michelle Hollinger's book, "Are YouWorthy?" serve as your travel companion. In it, you will be safely guided through her relatable story of discovering, developing and demonstrating her own self-worth. Expect to be informed, inspired and enrolled in a new possibility of all that you are and all that you can and will ever be — worthy!"

Rev. Kevin Kitrell Ross
Senior Minister/CEO
Unity of Sacramento
Sacramento, CA

"What would you do if you knew you were worthy of all?" In her book *"Are You Worthy?"* Michelle effortlessly guides us in understanding that each of us is worthy just as we are. By embracing her words and personal stories, each reader will enter a necessary conversation with self to unravel the illusion of unworthiness. At this time in human history, there is a call for more beings who know their beautiful and inherent worth. This book will support you in answering that call."

Pastor Greg Stamper
Co-Pastor
Celebration Spiritual Center
Brooklyn, NY

"This book addresses a topic nearly everyone can use – how to crush the belief of unworthiness. It will help eliminate the "I'm not good enough" blocks so you can soar to heights previously unimagined. Get this book and more importantly practice the principles that it covers!"

Rev. James Trapp,
Senior Minister of Worship
Spiritual Life Center
Sacramento, CA
Former CEO of Unity Worldwide Ministries

ACKNOWLEDGEMENTS

These spiritual leaders are a part of my spiritual journey.
Thank you for saying "YES" to shining your light.
You helped redirect me to my worth.

Rev. Ed Bacon, Rev. Jean Batchie,

Pastor Yolanda Batts, Rev. Michael Bernard Beckwith,

Rev. Eric Butterworth, Rev. Tita Calzada,

Rev. Bill Cameron, Rev. Johnnie Colemon

Rev. Luzette Diaz, Rev. Karen Epps,

Rev. Jackie Hazel, Rev. Ike,

Rev. Chris Jackson, Rev. Sherri James,

Rev. Elizabeth Longo, Rev. Gaylon McDowell,

Rev. Sheila McKeithen, Rev. Anna Price ,

Rev. Kevin Kitrell Ross, Pastor Greg Stamper,

Rev. Sylvia Sumpter, Rev. Charles M. Taylor ,

Rev. Sheree Thompson, Rev. James Trapp ,

Rev. Mary Tumpkin and Rev. Derrick Wells

TABLE OF CONTENTS

INTRODUCTION

U nworthiness is preventing people from living their best life. Even though procrastination, fear, self-sabotage and other excuses are fueled by a case of undiagnosed unworthiness, people don't talk about it or explore its impact because many don't realize that it's a factor in their lives.

It's subtle and can go undetected for years, a lifetime even, because its primary symptom is mediocrity; a widely accepted ailment masked by good jobs that pay the bills without fulfilling souls, and comfort zones that really aren't comfortable because they're constructed and maintained by playing small and settling for less.

Writing my book *Worthy,* in early 2018, changed my life because it pierced the unworthiness that had been blocking me from being my best self. I was shocked to discover that unworthiness was the culprit because I'm an intelligent, hard-working, college-educated woman with strong spiritual beliefs. Because unworthiness is so imperceptible, it was incredibly effective at numbing me to its existence. And if you can't identify a problem, you can't solve it.

In my desire to finally understand what was blocking me and why, I realized unworthiness was the culprit and that my childhood held clues to how it was ruling my adult life. Growing up, my experiences included multiple tragedies and dysfunction which, in retrospect, were clearly factors in me feeling unworthy. Discovering how it originated helped me figure out how to dissolve it, but not just for myself.

I share my unworthiness journey to help others consider how and why some of their childhood experiences impacted how they view their worth. But more importantly, I share it to help others know regardless of the circumstances, reconnecting to their innate worth is liberating and necessary to change their lives.

THE WORTHY PRAYER

I am worthy.
Just because I am.

No one else defines my worth.
No circumstance limits my worthiness.
I reclaim the power of my worthiness through forgiveness.

I am worthy.
Just because I am.

I am worthy of the very best life has to offer.
I am worthy of love, health, prosperity, peace and joy.
I unleash the energy of my worthiness
and it shapes my journey.

I am worthy.
Just because I am.

I am worthy of harmonious relationships.
Because they reflect the relationship I have with myself;
I honor me with love, compassion and respect.

Are You Worthy?

I am worthy.
Just because I am.

Every day I embrace my worth.
I intentionally celebrate my worthiness.
I cherish my worth with thoughts, words and actions.

I am worthy.
I use my voice.

I am worthy.
My opinion matters.

I am worthy.
I do not play small.

I am worthy.
Settling is not an option.

I am worthy.
I face my fear.

I am worthy.
Just because I am.

MY
UNWORTHINESS
MASTERCLASS

Understanding where my unworthiness originated was helpful to understanding how to deal with it. Before I could fully embrace the truth - I AM WORTHY - I had to journey back to my childhood and the seeming nonstop violation of my young body to get a better understanding that the unworthiness began there. I went back not to rehash the past, but to realize how the unworthiness began so that it can be ultimately be healed.

It began when I was around 7 or 8-years old and my late brother sexually assaulted me. I don't remember which happened first, but around the same time I was also fondled by an adult cousin on a fishing trip.

And then there was the carefree summer day of playing outside with my little brother and our friends, going to the Frozen Cup Lady's House and the neighborhood park when the owner of the corner store placed his hand on one of my newly sprouted breasts.

As a teen, I was molested by an uncle whose public persona oozed charm and charisma, successfully masking his uglier private identity. Adolescence and young adulthood brought more sexually inappropriate encounters with strangers – out jogging and a fellow jogger grabbed my behind; while studying at the gigantic FSU library, a guy parks himself directly across from me to masturbate.

A few years into my marriage, a man got out his car, in traffic, to touch me as I waited outside of the bank for my husband to pick me up. Stopped at a red light one evening when a car full of young men pulled up next to me. After trying unsuccessfully to get my attention, one exits the car to try to open my door, which thankfully, was locked.

At one point I remember thinking I must have had a "try me" sign on my forehead because of the serial encroachments. (I now realize that feeling **EXTREMELY** unsafe in the world and *expecting* to be assaulted radiated energy that sick men picked up on, but that's another book.)

Beyond the violations, my mother's death when I was 11 impacted my sense of unworthiness in ways I would not understand until I became a mother. The milestones a girl experiences – the start of her period, boyfriends, first dates and heartbreaks, graduations, move-in day at college – can be made smoother by a mother's energy. Living through each one without her while witnessing others bask in their mothers' presence amplified the emptiness, which had unexpressed grief and unworthiness lurking all through it.

My father's absence from my life resulted in significant daddy/daughter issues that shaped how I saw myself even though I wouldn't admit it; really couldn't admit it because I didn't realize the impact of growing up without him until my unresolved daddy stuff showed up in my marriage.

Poverty was also a factor in the unworthiness that took root during my childhood. I recall being pissed off whenever I had to buy powdered instead of regular milk with our food stamps. At school, seeing classmates with better things always reminded me that we didn't have enough money and I learned to not ask for things I knew my mother couldn't afford. My young mind associated poverty with shame and my beliefs about lack, limitation and expecting to never have enough followed me into adulthood. (I eventually learned poverty is a mentality that *needs* unworthiness in order to be sustained, yet another book.)

Although we had lots of wonderful experiences and beautiful memories, our family experienced an unusual amount of dysfunction and tragedy, including both my eldest brothers dying in violent deaths years apart, one at the hands of my beloved grandfather six months after Ma died.

As is the case in many families that simply didn't realize it was important, none of these heartbreaks was discussed and certainly never addressed therapeutically. That's just wasn't how we navigated major issues. When you don't know what you don't know, you do the best you can with what you do. Consequently, the pain, confusion, grief, sadness and ultimately the sense of unworthiness they generated were internalized and unwittingly left to roam freely and shape the way I saw myself and the world.

Years of spiritual and personal development prevented the underlying unworthiness from manifesting itself into any major dysfunction. What it did manifest, however, was a persistent belief that I was never enough. Never good enough, smart enough, confident enough, courageous enough. And because I never felt like I was pretty enough, I was shocked to be voted "most attractive" in high school.

Unworthiness blinds you to what is visible to others' eyes. It also fostered an immobilizing fear that held me rigidly in place and prevented me from reaching potential that dangled before my eyes.

I would not realize it for many, many years, but unworthiness was the underlying culprit that had me turning down my brilliance to appease others and being obsessed with what they thought of me. I said "yes" to keep the "peace" and buried my head in the sand to avoid speaking up about situations I had a right to confront. Self-sabotage could have been my middle name because while I felt capable of achieving certain goals, that "not good enough" syndrome made sure I did not.

Unworthiness did a number on me for a very long time because of how lowkey it is. Because of the spiritual work I'd immersed myself in, which included learning to forgive and understanding the power of my thoughts, I was convinced I was healed and capable of manifesting the life of my dreams.

Except I wasn't because a lingering unknown factor was frustrating my efforts to show up fully in my own life and be everything I'm here to be. It felt like an invisible elephant was always lurking nearby, blocking me from doing me. But because I couldn't see it, I couldn't address it.

The part of me that knew there had to be a better way kept me immersed in spiritual development in and out of church. I read self-help book after self-help book and attended seminars and conferences in the ongoing search for the elusive solution to whatever was preventing me from being the best Michelle I could.

Therapy was helpful, but never really freed me from this unidentified thing that kept me playing small. I really wanted to figure things out because I refused to live my entire life unwittingly ruled by mediocrity; ultimately taking my dreams and potential to the cemetery.

Thankfully, the part of me that knew there was a better way connected me to Ann Charleus, my former business consultant, who challenged another unworthiness-fueled habit of mine - a tendency to undercharge for high quality services and products. Because I was also tired of my undercharging pattern, when she asked, "Michelle, what's up with the low prices," I immersed myself into three days of silent solitude to find the answer.

A deeply spiritual introspective process of prayer, meditation and journaling helped me fill in the color of the invisible elephant by exposing that big sucker as unworthiness lying beneath the surface of my life, subtly keeping me under its powerful spell.

Discovering its presence in my life opened my eyes to its presence in the lives of others. I discovered just how pervasive it is and that it's rarely discussed because we don't recognize that even when things appear to be well and the bills are being paid, unworthiness can and does block us from being, doing and having more.

When you don't know what you don't know, you do the best you can with what you do. But what if knowing more about the topic of unworthiness can open the door to your best life? What if delving into it leads you to the worthiness that can set you free? What if by doing your work, you can change your life?

Are you worthy? Read on so that your answer is a resounding "YES!"

WORTHY NOTES:

Are You Worthy?

_____

_____

_____

_____

_____

_____

_____

_____

_____

_____

_____

_____

_____

_____

_____

_____

_____

_____

_____

_____

_____

_____

_____

~~WOUNDED WORTHINESS~~
ILLUSION OF UNWORTHINESS

Doing the work to address what I initially called "wounded worthiness" resulted in my first book on the topic, *Worthy*. As my worth consciousness continued to expand, *Are You Worthy? Powerful Steps for a Resounding "YES"* emerged with even more profound awareness regarding the source of unworthiness, the realization that it's an illusion and effective ways to dissolve it.

I discovered just how pervasive unworthiness is and how it shapes lives that appear good to the naked eye; but feel lacking and unfulfilling to the people living them. I also discovered the liberating power of my worth and, for the first time in my life, what it feels like to stand confidently in that truth.

Writing the book planted me smack dab into my worth consciousness and I began to attract beautiful experiences that matched its energy. I also learned that as it relates to this conversation about worth, there is still so much more to discuss. More layers to peel back, more to discover, more to reveal. More importantly, I learned that as powerful as this discussion has been since writing *Worthy,* I'd only scratched the surface.

In one of his masterful sermons, I was captivated by Agape Spiritual Center's Rev. Michael Bernard Beckwith's use of a beautiful phrase called "spiritual buoyancy." He explained that as we evolve and move from one level of consciousness to another, we exist in a space that could feel like being lost or in limbo, but is actually a rich, divine atmosphere where we're kept afloat by the Universe, which is always supporting us.

What we do consciously while in that sacred space determines whether we revert to our old level of consciousness, which feels safe and familiar; or we step firmly into the awaiting higher consciousness fueled by spiritual practices like affirmative prayer, meditation and introspection.

Worthy is a beautiful book that propelled me into the "spiritual buoyancy" necessary to lift me even higher into worth consciousness, which manifested *Are You Worthy?*

My worth. Your worth. Our innate worth sits within us, pulsating with divine potential, poised only to bless. Allowed to flow as is, our worth draws to us health, happiness, abundance, harmonious relationships, authentic power and the goodness of life.

We cannot work on our worth because it is not something we can fix. We can only work on our *perception* of our worth. And because we're born with all the worth we'll ever get, we can neither add to nor subtract from our worth.

Ultimately, any belief other than **I AM WORTHY** is an illusion that we've embraced as real and that illusion is usually the result of our response to life experiences, that of course, run the gamut - from positive, nurturing experiences on one end of life's pendulum - to deep, traumatic events like sexual abuse and the loss of a parent on the other.

Many experiences are somewhere in the middle and even without malicious intent can still impact how we view our worth based on the meanings we attach. Triplets, for example, can grow up in the same household, with the same parents and same experiences but become three adults with three very different interpretations of their childhoods.

That's because we don't just live our experiences, we also assign them meaning. Attached to the meaning could be the belief that the experience defines our worth. Each time we respond to an experience by consciously or unconsciously assigning it meaning, we create a belief that gets added to our subconscious, which is the storehouse for our memories, attitudes, feelings and beliefs.

If the meaning we assign to the experience is good, we can internalize a belief that because the experience occurred, we are worthy. Conversely, if the meaning we assign to the event is bad, we can internalize a belief that because the experience occurred, we are unworthy.

And we do it all the time. We may not use the words worthy or unworthy, but we're often telling ourselves that we're not good enough, smart enough, thin enough, young enough, light enough, rich enough, etc. for _____ (fill in the blank.) It doesn't help that we're also bombarded with images and messages in the media that convince us we're unworthy unless we purchase certain products and services.

The truth is, good, bad or neutral, **no experience defines our worth**. Nothing outside of us does. Our worth stands alone. And our worth is good. Even positive life experiences do not define it, although they can be instrumental in preventing an illusion of unworthiness.

It is not the experience, but the *meaning* we assign to the experience, the way we think about it, how we judge it that leads to a belief and it is the BELIEF that we are worthy or unworthy that then becomes a filter our thoughts pass through, attracting to us subsequent experiences that match the belief.

Because of the repeated violations and the losses I experienced, I unconsciously believed I was unworthy. That belief became the foundation that informed what I manifested in my life. It fueled my procrastination, the fear, doubt and worry that immobilized me and the self-sabotage I pulled from my back pocket whenever it seemed I was about to succeed.

Are You Worthy? helps you determine whether an illusion of unworthiness has been blocking you from doing you. It will guide you through powerful strategies to dissolve the illusion while also providing tools and wisdom to reconnect with your innate worth, which has been there all along, waiting to be discovered and put to work.

Reconnecting to your worth and living from it is life changing and can manifest in an entirely different existence for you. If you do the work, prepare to experience a refreshing clarity about who you are and what you're capable of because you will discover (or rediscover) parts of yourself you may not realize are within you.

The reconnection is an inside-out process that requires **awareness** that it exists, an **intention** to reconnect with it and the determination to engage in a life-long **celebration** of it. It's a process you must navigate by yourself, for yourself because no one else determines your worth; a truth that will become increasingly apparent to you as your worth consciousness expands and your concern with others' opinions of you diminishes.

WORTHY NOTES:

_____

_____

_____

_____

_____

_____

_____

_____

_____

_____

_____

_____

_____

_____

_____

_____

_____

_____

_____

_____

_____

_____

_____

_____

_____

_____
_____
_____
_____
_____
_____
_____
_____
_____
_____
_____
_____
_____
_____
_____
_____
_____
_____
_____
_____
_____
_____
_____

Are You Worthy?

AWARENESS

Are You Worthy?

EVERYONE IS WORTHY

I am worthy. You are worthy. Everyone is worthy! Yes, even folk whose behavior leaves much to be desired. When people are disconnected from their worth, their conduct reflects it. So although this might be difficult to accept, even murderers and crooked politicians are – at their core – worthy beings. We all are. We were born that way.

Unworthiness operates on a spectrum. At its mildest, unworthiness impacts the individual by limiting their view of themselves and the world; manifesting as a mediocre life that has the potential for far better.

At its strongest, unworthiness is coupled with power and authority and becomes the basis for treating others horrifically by denying their rights, privileges or even taking their life; (i.e. George Zimmerman, Linda Fairstein, abusers, some police officers, some political leaders, etc.) Unworthiness is at the root of deviant behavior because it results from and fosters a significant disconnect from a person's worth consciousness, their true nature – which is inherently good.

On the other hand, people living from worth consciousness are not only aware of their own innate worth, but they also recognize others' worth and have no interest in inflicting harm upon them.

Are You Worthy? can help the individual interested in reconnecting with their worth consciousness experience the transformation it produces. When you change your beliefs about your worth, what you attract into your life also changes. Not because of any change to your unchangeable worth, but because of changes to the filter that surrounds it.

Think about the air conditioner in your car that's been keeping you and your passengers cool. One day you turn it on, and instead of cooling you off, it appears to be broken. You take it to the mechanic braced for a huge repair bill, but what he shows you instead is a filthy filter. He explains that while the unit in your vehicle is functioning properly, the filter was so clogged with dust and other particles that, as the air tried to flow through it, it was blocked.

At our core, our worth is pristine and functioning properly, but if the filter through which it flows is clogged with dusty beliefs, it can *appear* to be wounded and in need of repair. But it can't be repaired because there is nothing wrong with it. Cleaning the filter will allow what's already flowing to get through, circulate in and through your life and draw to you experiences that align with your worth.

When we are living from a distorted belief about our worth, we're living with an illusion of unworthiness. So, even as you consciously pursue a dream or goal, the illusion of unworthiness attracts results that match the distorted belief.

For example, you're applying for jobs that you more than qualify for, but you're scratching your head in frustration because you're not landing interviews or if you are, you're not being hired.

If you subconsciously believe you're not really qualified, that you're not good enough, and essentially, that you're not worthy of the jobs, those beliefs are attracting results that align with the beliefs regardless of what your resume says.

So the work is not to revive our worth because it was never dead or wounded or in any state that requires anything for it to function accurately. The work is to **clean our filter** and **dissolve the illusion of unworthiness** so that we see and experience our worth in its true form.

Gabrielle Union-Wade is a powerful example of living from worth. Although we've never met, she is one of my teachers, especially about worth. She is a beautiful, authentic, successful woman living a beautiful, authentic, successful life despite an experience that could have been used to justify a life of victimhood.

The actress, author, businesswoman and new mother speaks candidly about being raped at gunpoint when she was a teenager and generously shares the healing process she navigated to recover from the horrific experience. She has not allowed it to define her, and she moves through life with a rare transparency that includes an underlying intention to benefit others by revealing her truth.

With each revelation, Gabrielle seems motivated by a steely determination to be guided by her worth. She was guided by it at *Essence* Magazine's 2013 Black Women in Hollywood Luncheon, where she was deservedly presented the Fierce and Fearless Award for her renewed embrace of sisterhood following a self-disclosed period of mean girl antics. She was guided by it during the persistent journey to motherhood she and husband, Dwyane, shared on social media following the surrogate birth of their daughter; inspiring women who faced similar fertility challenges to explore other options for having children. And she's guided by it as she cleverly uses her celebrity status as a divine platform loaded with lesson after valuable lesson for living an authentic life.

Like so many sexual assault survivors, Gabrielle could have bought into the illusion of unworthiness that often comes with being violated, which could have led to a belief that her subconscious mind accepted and the life she attracted might look a lot different than the one she so beautifully shares with the world.

Gabrielle Union-Wade's life reflects the worth that has existed within her since before she incarnated as Gabrielle Union. This wise woman knows there isn't an experience in the world that can define her worth. Not even her success. Nothing defines worth. It is what it is and what worth is, is good.

WORTHY NOTES:

Are You Worthy?

THE TRUTH
ABOUT WORTHINESS

W orthiness is such a loaded word. Many assume it should be relegated to self-help books for people who are depressed or suffering from low self-esteem. The truth is, far more people are dealing with worthiness issues than you might believe. Even people who appear to have it all together experience worthiness issues.

Let me clarify. When I say worthiness issues, the issue is with a person's *perception* of their worthiness. There's nothing wrong with their worthiness, nothing wrong with their worth. It's their illusion of unworthiness that's the issue.

And it's subtle. Like carbon monoxide, a person's illusion of unworthiness is sightless and odorless but potentially lethal. We don't realize how it is impacting us until its lowkey pattern of mediocrity or dissatisfaction shows up one time too many and something guides us to figure out what's really going on. An experience resonates deeply enough to stir up the energy of our worth consciousness, illumine the illusion and compel us to examine how we're living.

There are so many common scenarios that people settle for because they don't feel worthy enough to experience something better. Going to jobs they hate, remaining in toxic relationships, undercharging for products and services, dimming their lights to "keep the peace," saying "yes," when they really want to say "no," and more.

And in the age of social media, our collective illusion of unworthiness has been exploited; got us believing our obsessive participation with Facebook, Instagram and Twitter makes us worthy. Hogwash. The preoccupation with these external fixations only strengthens the illusion of unworthiness because becoming reacquainted with our worth is an inside-out job.

The illusion of unworthiness seems harmless because it lurks just beneath the surface, blocking us in ways we cannot see with the naked eye. A very gifted artist friend of mine, for example, was doing her thing, using her talent and putting her work out there. When she entered a prestigious art show, her illusion of unworthiness reared its head. Other artists with comparable art had priced their work at far higher prices – and their art was selling and selling briskly.

She, on the other hand, had priced her work far too low by charging rates that really were not in alignment with the sheer beauty and brilliance of her artistic gift. She initially blamed other factors for choosing to sell her art so cheaply; but when she got real with herself, she was willing to admit that her perception of her worth, an illusion of unworthiness, was the culprit behind her choices.

Regardless of what religion teaches about "original sin" or any other belief to the contrary, everyone is born in a state of perfect worth. We create our own bliss when we allow that perfect worth to flow freely and manifest as our best life, showing up physically, relationally, financially, vocationally, spiritually, mentally, emotionally, socially and every aspect of our lives.

An illusion of unworthiness stifles the manifestation of our best life by suppressing the free flow of our worth. When it exists, the illusion impacts people differently. The common thread is its infiltration into our feelings, which act as a compass or an indicator that informs us where we are in relation to our worth. And if we're not living from our worth, our feelings let us know when we're moving closer to it or further away.

That feeling you get when you go to the job you hate is an indication from your worth that you're out of its range. Feeling relaxed and inspired when around certain people means they're reminders of your worth. Conversely, feeling anxious when you're around other people could mean they contribute to your illusion of unworthiness.

Piercing the illusion of unworthiness allows the energy of your worth to flow through the opening, reconnecting you to your worth consciousness. Reacquainting yourself to it manifests experiences that align with its power.

WORTHY NOTES:

Are You Worthy?

FACING THE ILLUSION

Regardless of how we acquired it, living from the illusion of unworthiness impacts the quality of your life because it colors your view of who you really are and your true capabilities. Thing is, if you don't know you're living from an illusion, you can spend your entire life living beneath your true potential, believing you were doing the best you could. The illusion distorts your view of what's possible and what you're divinely designed to accomplish.

The illusion of unworthiness is clearly at the root of major life issues like addictions, poverty, abusive behavior and debilitating relationships; however, the illusion is also the imperceptible culprit when life is "normal," but far from fulfilling. You do not have to be in distress, dealing with a traumatic situation or suffering from low self-esteem to create and be impacted by the illusion. Life can be good, with all basic needs being met.

Here's the thing, you don't have to be sick to want optimal health, and you don't have to be poor to desire wealth and financial abundance. You don't need to be facing divorce to want a more harmonious, healthier relationship, and you don't have to be unemployed to crave an opportunity to express your unique gifts and talents. If you're living from the illusion of unworthiness, however, accepting substandard conditions feels like the right thing to do because when things are "normal," we've been convinced it's ungracious to want more. And sometimes, people live from the illusion because they don't realize they have a choice.

The illusion impacts people differently. Many of us have had experiences that foster an illusion of unworthiness. Various experiences — some major, some minor - that we assigned meaning became long-held beliefs that we're unworthy.

Abuse of any kind, abandonment, rejection, bullying, rigid expectations from parents and other authority figures as well as societal norms that minimize the value of certain groups impact on our beliefs about the self that can result in an illusion that we are not worthy.

Because what we focus on expands, the work to dissolve the illusion rests not on analyzing it, but on shifting your relationship with it. To only focus on how it blocks you from living from your worth would merely bring you more experiences that match the distorted belief that created it. Identifying how the illusion of unworthiness shows up in your life is necessary, however, the way you engage it beyond that point plays a significant role in your ability to dissolve it.

Prior to beginning the work to dissolve the illusion, however, it's worth (pun intended) considering the role an enormous institution like religion plays in your ideas about worthiness.

WORTHY NOTES:

Are You Worthy?

THE ROLE OF RELIGION

Religion holds a dominant, inescapable presence that impacts virtually every aspect of life, including the perception of worth; *especially* the perception of worth. Your concept of God affects your concept of your worth. If you believe God is a judgmental man in the sky keeping track of your every sin and making plans to punish you for them either now or in the hereafter, you might find it very hard to believe you were born worthy, you're worthy right now and you will remain worthy, regardless of anything you might have done.

For women, patriarchal religious doctrine could make it hard to accept that women and men are equally worthy, but we are.

I understand how delicate this conversation about religion is, specifically Christianity. Many Christians believe their religion is not only best for them, but also for everyone else and do not take kindly to people questioning any aspect of it. I share my thoughts on it not to be disrespectful, but to inform others who might be weary of its dogma but afraid to explore its impact on their lives, that a significant aspect of reclaiming your worth is owning your right to question and analyze anything that affects your perception of it. And that includes religion.

Because it was more instrumental in my journey from unworthiness to worthiness than I realized, I share my personal relationship with religion, how it impacted my perception of my worth and what I ultimately embraced that aligns with the truth. My journey will resonate with some of you. For others, it might sound crazy and blasphemous. I invite you to take what helps and toss the rest.

My family did not grow up immersed in religion and for reasons I did not understand until much later, I am grateful for that fact. My maternal grandfather was a dynamic Church of God in Christ preacher who retired from the ministry before I was born. Growing up, I can count on one hand the number of times we attended church. My brothers, cousins and I took pictures in our Easter outfits every year. My most vivid Easter memory was when my older brother, Tony, and I sat outside Antioch Baptist Church in Brownsville (Miami) during the service, munching on the candy we bought with the money we were supposed to place in the offering basket.

When I was around seven or eight, my mother took me with her to Cohen AME (African Methodist Episcopal) in Miami's Overtown neighborhood one Sunday. Ma had been sick and, now recovered, she stood in front of the church to share her testimony. The adults cheered her on, many standing, clapping and shouting, especially when she paused to gather herself. I'd never seen anything like it and watching her get emotional made me emotional too. She chuckled a little when she rejoined me on the pew; squeezing my hand and whispering in my ear, "I didn't mean to make you cry."

I have vague memories of my mother receiving a small red cloth in the mail from a man named Reverend Ike. I had no idea what the cloth was for but knew prayer was somehow involved. When I learned, many, many years later what his powerful ministry was about, I really wished my mother had had the opportunity to worship with him in person.

Undoubtedly, the most religious person in our family was my Aunt Vira (pronounced Viry), my mother's sister, elder by a couple of years. She and my mother were very close, and she visited our house often. Each time she did, she was carrying her bible in one hand; a fashionable designer purse in the other. Aunt Vira used to be dressed to the nines, too. She always wore heels and either a pretty dress or a skirt with a matching top. Hair always on point and perfectly applied make-up matched the loving, jovial energy that always proceeded her. I adored Aunt Vira.

When I was around eight or nine, Aunt Vira's youngest daughter, my cousin/best friend Charlotte, was the same age and my baby brother, Nealon, was four. Concerned that we were not attending anybody's Sunday school and therefore not learning anything about Jesus and the Bible, Aunt Vira coaxed the three of us into playing a game with $20 going to the winner. She gave us a Bible and a few days to memorize its books. With the money as incentive, we got busy studying. I won, Charlotte took second and Nealon got an honorary mention and five bucks just for trying.

A couple of years later, my mother's illness returned and took a turn for the worse. While she was hospitalized, I was at Aunt Vira's and Nealon was at Aunt Maxine's, one of my mother's younger sisters whose son, Venice, was a couple of years younger than my brother. The two were buddies and were together frequently.

Ma died on November 8, 1974. I was 11-years old and at Aunt Vira's house when the telephone rang early the next morning. Lying in one twin bed while Charlotte slept in the other, I heard Aunt Vira outside the closed door when she broke the news to her teenage daughter, Tawanna. I jumped up, confused, and started crying. No one talked about her illness and I had no idea my mother was that sick. The morning felt weirdly surreal. Before she left for the hospital, Aunt Vira reminded us it was a Saturday and Charlotte and I had chores to complete. Tawanna supervised.

Ma knew she was dying so she had taken care of everything beforehand, including making arrangements with Aunt Vira to assume custody of Nealon and me. Apparently, my aunt agreed to do so before my mother died, but shortly after Ma transitioned, changed her mind based on some dynamics that I'm still not clear about.

Years later when I became an adult, a wife and a mother, I tried to consider what might have prompted Aunt Vira to renege; thought about the myriad responsibilities adults manage and without knowing for sure what transpired, I forgave her.

My aunt passed away in the early 90s. Years before she transitioned, I lived with her briefly while in high school. I have fond memories, especially of the early mornings when I'd be running late, and we'd hop in her red Camaro to race down the city bus. We never discussed her broken promise. I only share the story to help explain my early relationship with religion and the conflicting ideas my young mind began to develop about it. It was my first time seeing church folk say or do things I didn't understand. The next would be when my grandfather decided we should remember our mother as she was when she was alive, and Nealon and I were not allowed to view her body or attend the funeral.

We ended up living with Aunt Maxine, Uncle Delton and their four children, Derrick, Mel, Sherri and Venice. We never attended church, which was fine with me. I recall Aunt Maxine once saying she wanted us to feel free to choose a religion that suited us when we became adults – a position I respect immensely.

I didn't entertain the idea of religion or church until I went away to Florida State University in 1981. Something was stirring in me and I sensed that being in church would sooth it, so I visited a few before joining St. Mary's Baptist Church near the FSU campus. Although I enjoyed the services, there was something I couldn't quite put my finger on that always left me feeling guilty, confused or aching for more.

I continued attending, but sporadically, eventually finding my way to a Church of God in Christ near my apartment. I was captivated by the loud, enthusiastic music, the amazing choir and the rousing sermons. That the congregation got "happy" with regularity was amusing, but frustrating because this happiness-inducing "Holy Ghost" was apparently familiar to many people - from my fellow college coeds to the senior citizens - everybody except me. I remember thinking there was something wrong with me or there had to be something I wasn't doing. I wanted to experience what everyone else was experiencing, so I clapped louder, stood and swayed. I closed my eyes like the older women and waited for the Holy Ghost to show up.

Weekly attendance became my norm. One Sunday, certain this was my lucky day, I stood up, clapped, sang along and although overcome with emotion, I could tell it wasn't the Holy Ghost. Other people were falling out, speaking in tongues, sweating and being surrounded by ushers to catch them when they collapsed. This Holy Ghost seemed to be a profound part of the religious experience. So how come it was skipping over me? Maybe I needed to join the church, I reasoned, so I made my way to the front when the pastor extended the invitation.

As I stood there, not a partier, hardly a drinker, but sexually active with my longtime boyfriend, something inside of me said if I joined that church, my entire life had to change. I quickly got an usher's attention and whispered to her, "I'm not ready," then walked out in the middle of the service and went home.

That was the last time I attended church in Tallahassee before returning to Miami in 1985. Graduation and marriage followed, and so did the inner stirring. Ex-hubby was nervous whenever we went to church because I would inevitably drag him with me down front to either receive prayer or join. We ended up becoming members at New Way Baptist church in Miami Gardens and it wasn't long before my big, tormenting questions started. Did heaven and hell really exist? What's up with sin, repenting and being saved? Where, exactly, was God and how was it possible for Him to not only hear millions of prayers, but answer them, too.

Still not a big partier or drinker, and now married, I didn't understand why I felt guilty following each sermon; and the confusion didn't let up either. I couldn't wrap my brain around the idea that by simply accepting Jesus as my personal Lord and Savior, I was "saved." If that's all there is to it and it's available to everyone, I reasoned that murderers and other people who intentionally inflicted harm on others could, by simply uttering a few words, be spared the condemnation that otherwise guaranteed them a place in hell. With that formula, people could "sin" all their lives but just before dying, accept Jesus and be guaranteed safe passage to heaven.

And speaking of heaven and hell, did God determine who got sent to burn based on one horrendous deed or could they commit that horrendous deed then perform dozens of good ones and go to heaven? What if the person had a violent street reputation, but while at home with his toddler son, was a doting father who taught him the alphabet and sign language? When I imagined my brother, Skip, a vicious ex-con and awesome daddy burning in hell based on the awful stuff he'd done, I needed to know whether his wonderful qualities were also a part of the equation. Did God weigh all that stuff? And what if Skip never got around to accepting Jesus?

That was enough for me. Skip was murdered on July 11, 1989 and I decided soon after his funeral that because hell didn't make sense, I would no longer concern myself with it. And when I heard, years later, the Pope himself said publicly that heaven and hell are not places, but states of mind, I was done. After trying in vain to feel more at ease at New Way by becoming involved in volunteering and activities, I stopped going altogether.

At some point after giving up on church, I was flipping through a magazine or newsletter and saw a prayer that resonated with me so deeply I cut it out and stuck it in my pocket. I read it a few more times and eventually misplaced it. By this time, I'd discovered a book called *You Can Heal Your Life* by Louise Hay that I devoured. Very spiritual, it focuses on the power of forgiveness, healing, self-approval and self-love. I was blown away that Louise Hay had healed herself of cancer by using the power of her thoughts, forgiveness, spiritual work and nutrition.

Other spiritual books began to line my shelves and Susan Taylor's "In the Spirit" column was also feeding my soul. It was a major reason I looked forward to *Essence* magazine each month and was always the first thing I read because her message centered on self-care, loving yourself and each other, authenticity, discovering your purpose, giving back – meaningful topics that resonated with my core.

In 1994, I was working as the manager of the Florida Foster Care Review Project. One day my boss, Julia Cope, and I were in my office chatting when the conversation turned to why we'd stopped attending church. Although she's Caucasian and I'm African-American, we'd both had similar experiences and many of the same unanswered questions. Julia got excited when she recalled a recent discussion with a dear friend who told her about a different kind of church with a pastor who "was full of himself," but also deeply spiritual and skilled at helping "seekers" make sense of religion.

"Look, if you stand right here, you can see it," Julia said from behind me as she literally turned my head to see the tall white building with the word UNITY atop a few miles southeast of the office.

Intrigued, I stopped by during my lunch break. I had no idea whether the church was open, but my intuition said to find its exact location so I'd know how to get there on Sunday. The church was closed, but not the bookstore. As soon as I entered, the energy, the peacefulness, the subtle smell of incense felt welcoming and familiar. The cashier looked up from the glass display and smiled.

"Let me know if you need any help."

I was mesmerized. The shelves were lined with books, many of which I had at home, and the eclectic jewelry displayed throughout the shop were pieces I would wear. Spirited artwork, candles and other earthy merchandise made time stand still in this surreal space, then one book caught my eye. Propped on the shelf with its full title visible, not shelved like the other books was *You Can Heal Your Life*. By now, I was covered in goose bumps with tears spilling from my eyes. A few deep breaths helped me regroup, and after browsing a little more, I bought incense and a box of *You Can Heal Your Life* inspirational cards before returning to my office.

I could hardly wait the few days before Sunday arrived. Walking into the foyer of Unity on the Bay felt like Deja vu. There on the wall was a big, beautiful tapestry with a prayer stitched on it. I knew immediately it was *the* prayer, the one I'd seen in the magazine.

The light of God surrounds us.

The love of God enfolds us.

The power of God protects us.

The presence of God watches over us.

Wherever we are, God is.

And all is well.

Confirmation! I was home. Not only was this very soothing prayer (The Prayer of Protection) on the wall, we also recited it at the end of the sermon. That was the first time my daughters Alexandra (8), Stephanie, (18 months) and I visited the church I would attend for over 20 years. Everything about it felt right, especially the guided meditation, preceded by a beautiful song that deepened my interest in understanding the power of my thoughts.

Our thoughts are prayers,

And we are always praying,

Our thoughts are prayers,

Listen to what you're saying,

Seek a higher consciousness,

A state of peacefulness,

And know that God is always there.

And every thought becomes a prayer.

Rev. James Trapp, the "full of himself" pastor of this beautifully diverse congregation was full of grace, wisdom, gentle humor and spiritual brilliance that grew the congregation from a few hundred when he was appointed as its senior minister in the early-90s, to more than a thousand in no time.

I'd finally found a church with a message that made sense to me at one of the oldest New Thought ministries in existence. For once, I felt wonderful in church and like I was floating when I left. I felt empowered and relieved to know God was not the bearded old man in the sky, but an ever-present, all loving power, always flowing, always blessing, always good. I gained a new understanding and deep appreciation for Jesus, our Way Shower who encouraged us to do everything He did and more.

My misgivings about worshipping Jesus as God also served as a source of confusion, so to learn that Christ wasn't his last name, but the state of divinity within Him that He ascended to and that it also exists within us SET ME FREE. Learning that Jesus was passionately interested in teaching us to love radically and unconditionally SET ME FREE.

Learning that God works through me and that my thoughts created my experiences filled me with an excitement I didn't even know existed. I'm a thinker. Always have been. Always will be. It's one of the reasons Unity and New Thought resonated so deeply with me. Borne from Christianity, Unity and New Thought deviate from the rote beliefs handed down by men and embrace the principles Jesus demonstrated. As such, Unity is based on five principles, which deepened my understanding and appreciation for New Thought even more:

1. God is absolute good, everywhere present. There is only one Power, one Presence, God.

2. Human beings have a spark of divinity within them, the Christ spirit within. Their very essence is of God, and therefore they are also inherently good.

3. Human beings create their experiences by the activity of their thinking. Everything in the manifest realm has its beginning in thought.

4. Prayer is creative thinking that heightens the connection with God-Mind and therefore brings forth wisdom, healing, prosperity and everything good.

5. Knowing and understanding the laws of life, also called Truth, are not enough. A person must also live the Truth that he or she knows. We cannot NOT live these laws- they apply to everyone, all the time, whether we "believe" in them or not.

OMG! I fell in love with these principles. They made sense and placed the power to change my life smack dab in my lap! Unity on the Bay really helped me accept that I am made in God's image and likeness and God works through me.

I was introduced to praying affirmatively and taught that its purpose was not to get God to do anything. Affirmative prayers were for me – to raise my consciousness to a place where it aligns with the goodness of God. I also learned the Kingdom of God that other churches presented as this far off destination only accessible after death, is a sacred space within me accessible through meditation and prayer. I learned that beseeching and begging prayers were unnecessary since God knows all and is all and doesn't need me telling God what to do. I could breathe now. This all made sense. No more guilt or confusion.

Unity on the Bay became my spiritual home and while there, I became a prayer chaplain and worked in the children's ministry. Unity and the New Thought movement introduce me to a different understanding of God's omniscience, omnipotence and omnipresence, but *The Universe is Calling,* by late Unity minister and author Rev. Eric Butterworth was the book that anchored my realization of God's presence WITHIN ME, which totally transformed my relationship with religion and with God.

His brilliant explanation helped me understand why the traditional concept of God is incredibly antiquated and disempowering. He referred to it as the "confused attitude toward God that prevails through the world of religion." He is, of course, referring to the idea of God as a man in the sky.

Butterworth was a metaphysical bible scholar and I found his historical analysis of religion's evolution an extremely helpful guide to understanding such a complex and delicate subject. (I was so grateful for his teachings that, much to my family's confusion, I flew to New York to attend Butterworth's memorial service when he transitioned in 2003.) Interestingly, Maya Angelou, who visited Unity on the Bay several times over the years, delivered Butterworth's eulogy.

Several years after Rev. Trapp left Unity on the Bay to accept the role as CEO of Unity Worldwide Ministries, the need for a different experience emerged. I began watching Rev. Michael Bernard Beckwith via the live streams from the Agape International Center's powerful and enlightening Sunday services.

I also began attending the Universal Truth Center in Miami Gardens, a powerful New Thought church. One of the most fascinating aspects of this powerful center is that the ndation for Better Living, the organization to ɪelongs, was founded by an African-American Johnnie Colemon was one of the first Blacks to become an ordained Unity minister in 1956 and promptly founded Christ Universal Temple, a Chicago-based megachurch that is still going strong under the leadership of Rev. Derrick Wells.

Learning this was significant because my every encounter with Black churches had been the traditional religious, "God-in-the-sky" experience that preached unworthiness as a virtue. Rev. Johnnie, as she was affectionately called, created a space where her predominantly Black congregation could have an empowering, transformative spiritual experience.

Like the revolutionary Rev. Ike, whose Science of Living ministry taught ideas that were diametrically opposite fundamentalist beliefs that promote separation from God, Rev. Johnnie made it clear that people have the power to change their lives and could do so by embracing a new idea about God and understanding the significance of their thoughts.

I'm now a member of Celebration Spiritual Center in Brooklyn. Entering this beautifully diverse, energetic, sacred space felt like a full-circle moment, so reminiscent of my first day at Unity on the Bay. Pastor Greg and Pastor Yolanda provide a powerfully transformative brand of New Thought that fuses sacred wisdom, spiritual brilliance, teaching, yoga, meditation and the most soulful New Thought music I've ever heard.

So, you're probably wondering, what does this have to do with worthiness? My short answer is everything. The longer answer centers around the confusion I felt back in the day when I heard more than one preacher shout, "Lord, I know I'm not worthy of your goodness, but," or "how could a sinner like me, ever deserve your mercy?" And, they preached, even though we owed Him big time because He gave us His only begotten Son, there was nothing we could ever do to repay Him.

When the preachers would shout that we weren't worthy of God's goodness and the Amen corners agreed, I always felt a little something-something in my belly but didn't know why. And I never could turn to my neighbor and say any of the negative, self-minimizing comments they'd tell us to say. When they taught that, as born sinners, we would **always** fall short of the glory of God, I felt lost.

That message didn't square with us being made in God's image and likeness and frankly, never resonated with me. At all. I think that's where some of the guilt used to come from. I could never agree with the sentiment that God was a jealous god intent on punishing his creations and I felt like as a Christian, I was supposed to accept it all. I never felt comfortable asking questions and got the very strong impression that doing so was disrespectful and blasphemous.

Oprah apparently felt the same way. On an episode of Super Soul Sunday where her guest was Richard Rohr, a priest and author of *The Universal Christ,* she shared a story about hearing a contradictory message while in church when she was 22.

"I was sitting in a church service listening to a really fine minister talk about God being angry and jealous and in the same breath saying omnipotent, all caring, all loving…How is that possible, God, that you're both angry and jealous and also omnipotent, all loving and caring," she wondered to herself. Like so many people who are terrified of even noticing the disparity, let alone forming a query about it, Oprah said she thought, "you're going to get struck in the eye for that, just for asking the question."

It also concerned/confused me that the very same religion slave masters used to destroy my ancestors' awareness of their inherent worth; the Christianity that kept them obedient with threats of hell, was continuing to enslave people by preaching duality – that we're separate from God – and suffering is good because rewards (heaven) happen when you die.

One of Fr. Rohr's other criticisms of what he called "Kindergarten Christianity," is how it discourages thinking. Reconnecting to your innate worth requires doing things differently, and that includes thinking in a new way. It involves questioning authority and re-examining stodgy old beliefs that could unwittingly promote unworthiness. More than anything, it demands a courageous willingness to relinquish allegiance to widely accepted practices that feel affirming but actually cultivate mediocrity, a first cousin to unworthiness.

As it relates to owning your worth, aspects of religion are ripe for reassessment. The idea of a "devil" is absolutely necessary to reexamine if you're serious about reconnecting to your innate worth because everything about it is designed to make you think you're unworthy.

The idea of a "devil" reinforces unworthiness because it relies on you believing you don't deserve anything good, coupled with your persistent expectation for bad things to happen. Think about it, whenever you pursue a dream or are interested in doing something special, if you believe in the "devil," you're worried that this negative entity is lurking around the corner waiting to throw a monkey wrench into your plans. Why even bother trying to improve your life? Why even bother to live your life like you're worthy? Why even consider believing that things can be better for you? Why?

Could it be that the "devil" was concocted as a control mechanism to keep people in line? To keep them disconnected from their worth and therefore distanced from their ability to manifest better? It was certainly used that way to keep slaves from escaping to freedom.

Like other significant portions of the good book, the "devil" is an aspect of the Bible that is allegorical and not to be taken literally. Unfortunately, people have grown up hearing family members and trusted members of the clergy refer to it with such conviction that they've accepted it as a reality. And what you accept as reality, whether it actually exists or not, becomes real for you in the form of a self-fulfilling prophecy. You expect the "devil" to be busy derailing your plans, so naturally something happens to mess things up, which you point to as proof that the "devil" is real.

Nope, it was your belief that your plan would not work that guaranteed that it didn't. The "devil" represents your negative thoughts, which throw a monkey wrench into your plans by generating experiences to match their negative energy. Believing in a "devil" while trying to dissolve unworthiness will keep you in a revolving door of mediocrity and the unrelenting, exhausting belief that you can do absolutely nothing about it.

Another counterproductive religious notion is the idea of "favor." You have undoubtedly heard or perhaps even used the phrase, "favor ain't fair," which seems to mean God blesses someone even though they don't appear to deserve it. They've been "favored" by God and because no one clearly understands how or why, the only feasible explanation is, "favor ain't fair."

Under the circumstances that this traditional "favor" is doled out, it really ain't fair. It implies that if you need a blessing, there's really nothing you can do to receive it because it's up to an external, capricious god to determine who will be favored.

According to this formula, God's criteria are unclear because someone who's been busting their behind to achieve success can get nothing and folk who have been chilling and expecting something for nothing can be the lucky recipient of God's favor.

But what if, in this context, favor has a different, less arbitrary meaning?

Before I explain, I invite you to consider that for many words there is a difference between how Webster's defines them and what they mean in the Bible. For example, "fear" in the Bible does not mean to be afraid, but to be in awe of, to have deep, abiding reverence for. To "fear God," therefore, means to hold God in maximum regard; to have your mind blown and your breath taken away by the sheer beauty, majesty and power of the Supreme Being.

But in the literal interpretation of scripture, many people assume that words in Webster's and words in the Bible share the same meaning; which brings me back to "favor."

Webster's says favor means, "to feel or show approval or preference for," as in a parent favoring one child over another. Many believe the scriptural meaning of favor is the same; as in God favoring one person over another. Ask someone how they're doing and you're likely to hear, "blessed and highly favored," implying they've received this preferential treatment from God.

The idea sounds encouraging but actually saps you of your power, an essential ingredient in reconnecting to your worth. To understand why requires an open mind, a willingness to at least consider that God isn't a man in the sky and assurance that you will NOT be struck by lightning for thinking in a new way.

The implication of religious favor is that someone has been singled out by God and God is playing favorites. Being "highly favored" also seems to include an obligation to be petty by rubbing your blessing in naysayers' faces; a practice exemplified in a message by an extremely popular pastor who encouraged grown folk to indulge in childish behavior which, apparently, is a common part of the favor experience.

"And of course, they're going to be upset. Of course, they're going to roll their eyes when you walk in the room…Of course, they don't like you. Of course, they resent you. They're frustrated because God preferred you…And the next time you run up on somebody who is looking at you all funny, say 'yeah, I know what it is. Go ahead and have all the attitude you need to because this is favor. And favor ain't fair,'" Pastor T.D. Jakes said in a message aptly called, "Favor Ain't Fair."

But what if favor isn't some unfair blessing bestowed upon you that you flaunt to your "haters," but is instead something already WITHIN YOU that, when activated, can guide you to your best life? And what if God equipped everyone with this sacred quality instead of only selecting certain folk to receive it?

The Revealing Word, a dictionary of metaphysical terms used by New Thought ministers, practitioners and students, defines favor as, "The orderly unfoldment in mind and body that results from meditation and prayer; a blessing that comes to us through obedience to Spirit. The bringing about of an inner spiritual strength, resulting in the development of all parts of mind and body."

Based on this definition, favor is a state of elevated consciousness WITHIN YOU accessed intentionally by praying and meditating; two spiritual practices that help you align with omniscience; the all-powerful, everywhere present God WITHIN YOU. Praying, meditating and the consistent use of spiritual tools like forgiveness, gratitude and changing the way you think create an inner shift, unleashing a spiritual strength that empowers you to manifest health, prosperity, harmonious relationships, inner peace and dreams with your name on them.

Far less popular than the traditional "blessed and highly favored" approach; but far more powerful because this approach does double duty by naturally repelling the fear, worry, doubt and other external factors that keep you from living the life you were born to live. This "favor" hangs out with your innate worth, so activating one typically leads to the activation of the other.

Reassessing the idea of favor, the devil and religion as a whole played a major role in dismantling the unworthiness that plagued my life. Finding Unity on the Bay and New Thought was a breath of spiritual fresh air. In retrospect, I see how my worthiness journey unfolded and I'm grateful for every single part. I see the connection between my childhood experiences with a family also looking for its religious truth, and my Holy Ghost search in Tallahassee. I see how my big religious questions attracted people, experiences and spiritual centers that guided me to the answers I needed.

My journey helped me to see that exploring the role religion plays is an essential part of reconnecting to your worth. As you chart your own worthiness journey, I encourage you to give yourself permission to ask the questions you always wanted to ask. Perhaps your inquiry will strengthen your religious practice and help you appreciate your religion more.

Or maybe you will find the courage to acknowledge that it doesn't. Either way, you deserve to experience a belief system that celebrates your worth.

WORTHY NOTES:

The Role of Religion

Are You Worthy?

PSEUDO WORTHINESS

As a society, we're navigating a collective illusion of unworthiness. It's the reason social media exploded in popularity and is showing no signs of letting up.

We're desperately searching for something to fix our illusions of unworthiness, which feels flawed, scarred and terribly incomplete because it's not real and is blocking the life-affirming vitality from our worth consciousness. If we're not aware of our innate worth and the consciousness that flows naturally from it, we can chase our tails by believing the illusion is real.

One significant factor perpetuating our illusion of unworthiness is seeing example after example of people becoming famous for questionable reasons. And because they have all the perceived trappings of success, we assume they're worthy of it we're not.

We experience the "woe is me" angst that comes from living a life where ends don't meet, the job is a pain and our relationships are inharmonious and draining. Wrapped in our misery is a strong belief that everyone else gets all the lucky breaks.

Our illusion of unworthiness seems even more real because it feels like we're really trying to get ahead. Problem is, we're trying to use an externally focused approach to something that only permanently responds to an inside-out method.

Some of the folk with all the perceived trappings of success are still dealing with worthiness issues because things are incapable of filling the void. Amidst all the busy external stimuli, the illusion of unworthiness festers.

Our innate worth has been there all along, but reconnecting to it requires **awareness** that it exists, an **intention** to reconnect with it and the determination to engage in a life-long **celebration** of it.

WORTHY NOTES:

WORTHINESS AND
SISTERHOOD/BROTHERHOOD

Worthiness and sister/brotherhood are naturally intertwined. Women and men have the power to impact each other's awareness of their worth. And our desire to either perpetuate another person's illusion of unworthiness or celebrate their worth is informed by our own worth consciousness.

It takes living from the illusion to perpetuate the illusion. Women and men living from the illusion participate in gossip, fear, judgement, doubt, cynicism, worry, abuse, blame and dishonesty.

Conversely, women and men living from their worth consciousness have compassion for their sisters and brothers living from the illusion. They are aware that they are more than their sister's/brother's keeper, they are their sister/brother. Women and men operating from their worth consciousness bless other women and men with ease and genuinely want to see them succeed.

One of the most beautiful results of reconnecting to our worth consciousness is the impact it has on the women, men, girls and boys in our lives. When we're living from our worth consciousness, we have a natural desire to help others live from theirs. And when we're mothers, fathers, aunts, uncles, grandparents or in any role where we influence young women, young men, girls and boys, we learn to proactively protect and cultivate their worth consciousness.

Additionally, if we're shifting from the illusion to worth consciousness, we begin to attract others living from worth consciousness into our space. Vibing with people aware of their worth is a powerful blessing. The energy flowing in and through this group is life changing because there's an expectation for growth, progress and an authentic, supportive vibe bolstering everyone's success.

If the group you spend the most time with spends most of its time gossiping, complaining, judging, etc., chances are a collective illusion of unworthiness is floating among you. All it takes is one person to reconnect with their innate worth for its energy to ripple throughout the group; likely resulting in one of two outcomes. It will either inspire the others to reconnect with their worth, or lowkey encourage them to find another group.

WORTHY NOTES:

_____
_____
_____
_____
_____
_____
_____
_____
_____
_____
_____
_____
_____
_____
_____
_____
_____
_____
_____
_____
_____

Are You Worthy?

_____

_____

_____

_____

_____

_____

_____

_____

_____

_____

_____

_____

_____

_____

_____

_____

_____

_____

_____

_____

_____

_____

_____

WORTHINESS
AND SOCIAL MEDIA

Facebook founder, Mark Zuckerberg, brilliantly predicted that social media would benefit from normative social influence, a type of collective social sway that leads to conformity. Social psychologists define it as "the influence of other people that leads us to conform to be liked and accepted by them."

Who knew we'd become so obsessed with something that literally involves being "liked?" Who knew how it would impact our illusion of unworthiness? Apparently, Facebook's founding president, Sean Parker, knows how damaging it is because a few years ago, he shared that neither he nor his children use social media.

Social media engagement is an example of a normative social influence that is so widely accepted and deeply entrenched that we look at anyone who is not on Facebook, Instagram, Twitter, etc. as though they have three green heads and a purple horn protruding from their nose.

Zuckerberg and his co-creators understood psychology and used it to hook people on their product. Parker, the company's former president, admitted that when they were working to get the social media giant off the ground in 2004, he and others sat around figuring out, "how do we consume as much of your time and conscious attention as possible?"

Their solution?

"…We need to sort of give you a little dopamine hit every once in a while, because someone liked or commented on a photo or a post or whatever. And that's going to get you to contribute more content, and that's going to get you…more likes and comments."

Their strategy worked. We're taking selfie after selfie in search of validation from external sources – friends and strangers on Facebook, Instagram, Twitter and other mediums. Think about it – we take a picture of ourselves, share it with a group of people (some of whom are complete strangers), and then we check to see what those people think about our picture we took of ourselves.

If that behavior existed back in the day, it would be akin to taking a polaroid photo and then standing on a corner, showing it to family, friends and strangers and asking them what they think.

Excessive social media engagement in general and the obsessive use of selfies specifically is viewed as normal because of such widespread acceptance. But just because something is accepted in mass does not mean it's healthy. Even the folks who created it eventually felt tremendous guilt about how successfully they were able to exploit our need for validation. Parker criticized the way the company "exploits a vulnerability in human psychology" by creating a "social-validation feedback loop."

For people walking around with an illusion of unworthiness, this social validation feedback places a band-aid on the illusion, making it feel and appear to be healed when it's not.

To some degree or another, most people have participated in this national selfie obsession that is now a normal part of our lives. It seems like such a fun, innocuous and cool way to connect with friends and family. So, what's the harm? Is it really unhealthy?

Yes, if what's floating behind the selfie is sadness, disappointment, frustration with your life, with who you are and what you're doing, professionally and personally.

Posting selfies and livestream videos result in a temporary high that comes along with the "likes" and positive comments, but it really does nothing to soothe the deep emotional and spiritual void we're seeking to fill. It's external validation and using it to feel good about yourself is like applying a bandage to a seriously infected cut without disinfecting it, then expecting it to thoroughly heal.

WORTHY NOTES:

Are You Worthy?

WORTHINESS AND
THE OPRAH EFFECT

I feel obligated to discuss Oprah Winfrey when examining the word 'worthy' because of the impact she has had on our collective psyche; specifically as it relates to an awareness of our innate worth and our need for validation.

Although in its early years her talk show's format was similar to the others, Oprah quickly realized the opportunity she had to positively impact society. Oprah shifted her show's format from destructive topics that pitted people against each other to spiritual topics that offered us wisdom, information and inspiration to live our best lives.

The phenomenal 25-year run of the Oprah Winfrey Show, the highest rated ever, is evidence that she effectively tapped into and soothed our collective need to be reminded of our worth. For an hour a day, five days each week, Oprah Winfrey used her platform to encourage us to dissolve the illusion by going deeper. She introduced us to spiritual geniuses like Iyanla Vanzant, Gary Zukav and Eckart Tolle, all of whom, in their own way, encouraged us to live from worth consciousness.

The end of Oprah's talk show in 2011 left a huge societal void that is, to some degree, being filled artificially by social media. She offers similar content on her network, but because her audience is more varied, and her bottom line demands it,

OWN's programming is designed to resonate with people at different levels of consciousness.

Rich, substantive shows like Super Soul Sunday, Queen Sugar, Black Love, Iyanla Fix My Life, Master Class and others align with the values of the Oprah Winfrey Show and provide viewers with the spiritual nudge her talk show did. Through her talk show and her network, Oprah Winfrey's role in the collective celebration of worth consciousness is a monumental accomplishment for which I am grateful.

WORTHY NOTES:

EVIDENCE OF
THE ILLUSION

The illusion of unworthiness shows up in various ways, impacting people differently. Below are a few common examples of how it appears in people's lives and its impact.

ABUSIVE RELATIONSHIPS

Being in an abusive relationship is a sure sign that the illusion of unworthiness is a factor in your life. While there are other dynamics at play, being in an abusive relationship means at some subconscious level, you feel you deserve the abuse or that you don't deserve better. Whether physical, sexual, emotional or psychological, it likely stems from unhealed childhood experiences involving abuse – either witnessed or endured. Enlisting the help of a skilled therapist might be necessary to help you navigate your release from victimhood.

DIMMED LIGHTS

You have what it takes to significantly improve your quality of life and you know what you should do to make it happen; however, whenever you begin to take the necessary steps, you stop. The reason? Someone close to you says or does something to indicate their disapproval in your attempt to improve yourself. A part of you knows you deserve to continue moving forward, but another part of you is concerned about losing the approval of people close to you, or worse, losing the people altogether. Marianne Williamson describes the situation brilliantly in her book, *A Return to Love*, when she says, "There is nothing enlightened about shrinking so that someone else won't feel insecure."

DESPISED EMPLOYMENT

You spend an enormous portion of your life working. Second to the amount of time you spend at home is the amount of time you spend at work. Why would you accept devoting so much of your journey to doing something you hate? The reason is your illusion of unworthiness has convinced you it's OK because it pays the bills. You've accepted that other people can find and live their calling, but not you. But what if finding and living your calling – that thing that has YOUR name on it is what you're supposed to be doing? Reconnecting to your worth will also clarify gifts and talents you might not realize you have. Some might be suited for your current employment, where you can bloom where you're planted. Or they might require you to begin planning your exit as you identify that career your worth demands you pursue.

NO RAISE OR PROMOTION

The qualifier here is that you feel you deserve to be paid more or elevated to a higher position. If under those circumstances, you have never requested a raise or promotion, it is very likely due to your illusion of unworthiness. You've had the internal conversation with yourself several times and end up talking yourself out of asking because of how you assume your employer will respond. Your assumption is based, not on how your employer values you, but in how you value yourself. And how you value yourself stems from your illusion of unworthiness.

CONSTANTLY CRITICAL SELF-TALK

We all talk to ourselves, all the time. We're talking to ourselves even when we don't even realize it. If you have not taken control of your thoughts, chances are the conversations you're having with yourself are negative. Instead of congratulating yourself when you've done well, you spend far more time criticizing yourself when you've messed up. Instead of expecting good, you expect the worse. You actively live up to the saying, "you're your own worst critic" because the illusion of unworthiness dictates that your thoughts and words about yourself match its low energy.

HAUNTED BY REGRET

We've all used poor judgment and made mistakes. We have all done something we wished we hadn't or not done something we wish we had. It's a part of the human dynamic. If you're constantly beating yourself up by playing a "coulda, woulda, shoulda" game, however, it's an indication you're living from the illusion and finding it hard to cut yourself some slack. Living from worth consciousness makes self-forgiveness possible and self-forgiveness provides space for new ideas, new goals and new opportunities to manifest.

PASSIVE AGGRESSIVE

Someone asks you to do something you don't want to do. Instead of refusing, you say 'yes' and then grumble your way through it. A co-worker invites you to attend an event you're not interested in. Instead of thanking them for the invitation and declining, you show up and your attitude is toxic because you didn't want to be there in the first place. Someone says something you don't like. Instead of expressing your displeasure to them, you gossip about them behind their back. All are examples of passive-aggressive behavior that stem from an illusion of unworthiness.

NOT SPEAKING UP

You have an idea about how to cut costs at work, improve productivity or enhance morale but instead of sharing during the staff meeting or even in an email, you remain silent. Or you apologize unnecessarily and frequently. You're unhappy about the choice of restaurant your mate chose, but you go anyway, silently kicking yourself for not suggesting someplace else. Your mother-in-law routinely says something blatantly disrespectful to you, but you say nothing to address it. The illusion of unworthiness makes these scenarios possible.

CHURCH GUILT

This is a biggie many people participate in for their entire life. The specific church, type of church or denomination you're currently attending might have been chosen for you years ago when you were younger based on tradition or other familial factors. Although you've outgrown it, however, you continue attending even though the message no longer suits you. Even though the discomfort, guilt or unidentifiable nagging feeling is your soul urging you to find something that aligns with your needs, you remain because you're afraid to "rock the boat," potentially upsetting family, friends, fellow parishioners, your pastor, etc. You may even have religious fears about what might happen to you when you die if you make a change more in alignment with your spiritual needs.

THE TOO GOOD TO BE TRUE SYNDROME

Because we're innately worthy, the energy of our worth can occasionally flow through an illusion of unworthiness and attract people or experiences that match its natural goodness. When that happens, however, if the illusion of unworthiness is still an issue, it can convince us it is too good to be true and the energy of the illusion repels the person or experience. For example, people who suddenly acquire large sums of money, like lottery winners, but subconsciously feel unworthy will find ways to unconsciously squander the money so that their experience matches the energy of the illusion. The syndrome is also a factor if the partner of our dreams appears in our life while we're under the spell of the illusion. A belief that you don't deserve a person like them can result in you unconsciously sabotaging the relationship.

WORTHY NOTES:

_____

_____

_____

_____

_____

_____

_____

_____

_____

_____

_____

_____

_____

_____

_____

_____

_____

_____

_____

_____

_____

_____

_____

Are You Worthy?

INTENTION

Are You Worthy?

YOUR PIERCING POINT

Recognizing that you've been living with an illusion of unworthiness is a huge, potentially life-changing deal. Many, many people never realize it and go their **entire lives** dimming their lights, settling for less and basking in mediocrity when they were capable of excellence. Recognition and acceptance are prerequisites to dissolving the illusion.

Sitting silently and honestly exploring your life and where it's not measuring up to your desires might be necessary to pinpoint where your illusion is appearing because although distress, turmoil, low self-esteem and the like usually co-exist with the illusion, their presence isn't required for an illusion of unworthiness to be a factor.

It's a subtle entity that exists just beneath the surface of your life, but it informs how you show up, how you make decisions and what you manifest. It's what Henry David Thoreau meant when he said, "the mass of men lead lives of quiet desperation." People are going through the motions of living, settling for less and accepting it as their lot in life when there is so much more available to them.

The illusion of unworthiness offers a powerful starting point for returning to your worth consciousness. The illusion shows up differently for everyone, but it's typically the area of your life where dissatisfaction lingers, often imperceptibly to others, but as a silent, pesky knowing to you. Because it's not visible to the naked eye, the people around you might not even be aware that you're dealing with it. YOU might not be aware.

Fear, doubt and worry are normal parts of life's journey, but if they crop up as insurmountable obstacles that keep you from moving forward, the illusion of unworthiness is a factor. Whether it's the job you hate, the unhealthy relationship, or the dreams you dismiss, a belief that you are not worthy of better is the underlying culprit.

What we focus on most expands, so you don't dissolve an illusion by focusing on it. Focusing on the illusion of unworthiness makes it appear stronger and it continues to attract experiences that align with it and the distorted beliefs that created it.

The illusion does, however, offer an entryway to your worth. Becoming aware of the illusion is akin to piercing it. And then beyond the piercing exists the pathway back to your worth. You travel the pathway by shifting your relationship with the illusion because, "When you change how you look at things, the things you look at change," a powerful quote attributed to the late spiritual genius, Wayne Dyer.

WORTHY NOTES:

Are You Worthy?

BEFRIEND THE ILLUSION

This suggestion to befriend your illusion of unworthiness might not make any sense whatsoever. Especially since the illusion is usually based on an experience to which you've assigned an "unworthy" meaning. But this is not a fight. To do battle with your illusion would be to create resistance, which is counterproductive because what we resist, persists.

Further, if you perceive your illusion of unworthiness as a totally external entity that just sort of randomly showed up in your life, then you essentially have no power over its presence. If you believe it showed up randomly, you would also be inclined to believe it must leave randomly, of its own volition.

In the meantime, you would still be living beneath its veil as it continued to block you from reveling in and living from your worth consciousness. Accepting that your illusion of unworthiness is an external entity over which you have no control places you squarely in the wishing and hoping arena, which is void of the power necessary for embracing your innate worth.

If, however, you recognize and can fully embrace that you created the illusion and allowed it to function, you are in the driver's seat. If you are willing to accept that the presence of the illusion actually served a purpose, you can reclaim your power and are on your way to dissolving the illusion and removing it from your consciousness.

The illusion was created from distorted beliefs in your subconscious mind. The distorted beliefs resulted from the meaning you assigned to life experiences. In her book, "Key to Yourself," psychologist Dr. Venice Bloodsworth described the subconscious as, "The storehouse of memory, the seat of habit and instinct, it is also the center of emotion, and its action is automatic."

The decisions we're making, the thoughts we're thinking, how we're showing up in our lives all flow from by the subconscious. Distorted beliefs residing within our subconscious form an illusion of unworthiness.

Identifying how the illusion is showing up in your life is a power move. When you get clear about the illusion-based experience you're living, it contains treasure for you to discover. Soften your perception of the illusion by viewing it as a temporary placeholder that prevented you from stepping into an experience prematurely, before you cleaned up the distorted beliefs in your subconscious.

Now that you realize, for example, that an illusion of unworthiness is a factor in you working at a job you hate, aspects of your worth will begin to awaken, and clarity is one of the greatest advantages. Dissolving the illusion and moving closer to your worth could arouse gifts and talents within you that are best suited for your current employment, allowing you to "bloom where you're planted," transforming a job you hated into one that fulfills you.

"When you change the way you look at things, the things you look at change."

Or, the energy from your worth consciousness will make it clear that you have no business being employed at your current job. And now that you know, you can develop a plan to secure employment that aligns with your worth consciousness.

In my case, my illusion of unworthiness showed up in the tendency to undercharge for services and products. The work to dissolve my illusion of unworthiness had to begin with me accepting that I created it. I had to own that I allowed it to exist until I authentically believed my services and products were worth more than the paltry prices I placed on them. And that meant working on my worth consciousness by affirming that I was born worthy, by forgiving others and myself, redefining my past, learning to validate myself and using gratitude to celebrate my worth.

Your eyes on these pages are proof you've already begun the process to dissolve the illusion or you would not have attracted this book into your life. Now that you're on the journey to reclaiming your worth, you're positioning yourself to no longer need the illusion and can dissolve it organically, from the inside-out.

Taking responsibility for the illusion places you in prime positioning to dissolve it. The next step to its dissolution not only empowers you, it allows the illusion to dissolve from your existence, clearing the space to be filled with energy from your worth consciousness.

WORTHY NOTES:

Are You Worthy?

STEP INTO GRATITUDE

B ehind the illusion of unworthiness is where the truth of your worth exists. It's always been there. It's powerful and pure, waiting for you to rediscover its existence. It's a rediscovery because you were aware of it when you were born.

Until they are taught otherwise, babies know their worth and their actions reflect that awareness. They're unafraid to explore their surroundings. They get their needs met by communicating (typically crying) in a manner that gets attention and results in someone feeding them, changing their diaper, coaxing a burp from their little body or being comforted with affection. (Babies who do not get these basic needs met are very likely to develop an illusion of unworthiness.)

Beyond infanthood, going from knowing your worth to living with an illusion of unworthiness results from life experiences you assign meaning that become beliefs that hang out in your subconscious mind and inform how you live, move and have your being.

The belief that you are not worthy results in a subtle illusion that attracts to it matching experiences or conditions that reinforce the belief that results in the illusion that brings more matching experiences or conditions – and the cycle continues.

The illusion of unworthiness masks mediocre circumstances. It justifies an existence that does not align with your worth consciousness and numbs you to the "is this all there is" mental whimper that greets you on Monday mornings. The feeling in your gut is divine discontent with a message for you to unpack. When left unexplored, however, divine discontent is often misidentified as the stress you've been convinced is a natural, unavoidable part of life.

Gratitude is the bridge from this muddied illusion to the clarifying energy of your worth consciousness. It may seem counterintuitive, but it is extremely effective because it allows you to reclaim your power from the illusion; the only thing keeping the illusion "alive." Even though it's subtle, the illusion of unworthiness casts a limiting pall over your life. Changing the way you look at it changes its presence and you change the way you look at it through gratitude.

In my example, gratitude helped me discover the true value of my services. The program I developed that prompted my business consultant to challenge my prices, "40 is the New 20, But Not the Way You Think," is full of blessings for women of a certain age. By piercing the illusion of unworthiness that prompted me to place an unacceptably low price on the initiative, gratitude helped me find my way into an atmosphere of enthusiasm about the program and rekindled my desire to finalize it and present it to an eager audience.

I am grateful for this amazing program. I am grateful for an opportunity to remind women over 40 of the tremendous inner resources, like wisdom, courage and tenacity they've accumulated over the years. I'm grateful to remind women who have beat themselves up because they have not yet found their purpose that dreams and goals they had at age 20 that continue to nag them are still there for a very important reason. Now is the ideal time for them to nurture their dreams and use the wisdom of their maturity to boldly manifest them in a way they could not possibly have done two or three decades ago.

If your illusion has you reporting to a job you hate, for example, take a moment to find at least one thing about the job for which you're grateful. Are you grateful that you have a job? Perhaps your co-worker is now a great friend. Has the job allowed you to put your children through college? Have a roof over your head? Put food on the table? There are likely additional aspects you're grateful for, so spend a little time considering what they are. Make a list.

Even if you ultimately leave this job for the job that aligns with your worth, finding reasons to be grateful for the current job weakens the illusion of unworthiness and immerses you into the heightened vibrational field of your worth consciousness, which attracts matching experiences and conditions. So whether you remain at your current job or leave for something better, gratitude positions you to manifest an experience that aligns with your worth.

If you're in an unhealthy relationship, finding something about the relationship, your partner or yourself to be grateful for loosens the grip of the illusion. How has the relationship blessed you? Are you stronger as a result? What strengths have you discovered about yourself as a result of being in the relationship? What opportunities to heal past hurts has the relationship presented you?

Gratitude could shift the energy in the relationship and improve it. If, however, you decide to leave the relationship, gratitude shifts your energy to a more empowered stance that allows you to manifest future experiences that align with your worth. And if you end it, dissolving the illusion of unworthiness and reconnecting with your worth BEFORE becoming involved in another relationship helps ensure no repeats of the previous relationship(s).

If you're constantly dimming your light to appease others, what have you learned about yourself? What's inside of the light you've been dimming? What's aching to be set free? Can you cultivate compassion from the dimming while transforming it to a more assertive approach to shining your light? Coming to the realization that you've been dimming your light is a reason to be grateful. So many people live their whole life so addicted to pleasing someone else they lose touch with who they really are and the full potential within them.

If you say "yes" when you'd really prefer to say "no," wrapped within your disease to please is a compassionate soul that needs permission to own its voice. Redirecting the direction of your pleasing from others to yourself is a reason to be grateful.

Going to a church that doesn't really feed your soul? Have you admitted you're attending for reasons that have nothing to do with your growth and development? Making a list of what you're grateful for about your church can shift the energy around the experience. It can also help you get clear about what you want in a church, resulting in you remaining there with renewed appreciation or confidently searching for a new spiritual home.

It's important that when piercing the illusion of unworthiness and identifying aspects for which to be grateful that you use generous doses of love and compassion. When we know better, we do better. Becoming aware of the illusion is a very significant step because of its subtlety.

Taking responsibility for the illusion and then using gratitude to reclaim your power immerses you into the energy of your worth consciousness. And once you begin living from your worth consciousness, brace yourself because your life will change.

WORTHY NOTES:

Step into Gratitude

Are You Worthy?

THE THOUGHT FACTOR

Humans think an average of 60,000 thoughts each day. Ninety percent of those thoughts are repetitive. We're thinking the same thoughts day in and day out. And of the thoughts we recycle through our minds each day, eighty percent are negative.

As it relates to reconnecting to your worth consciousness, your thoughts play a monumental role in the journey. And once you've reconnected with your worth, your thoughts are essential to the preservation of your worth consciousness.

What we think about ourselves is fueled by our worth consciousness, an illusion of unworthiness or somewhere in between. What you think about as you're shifting from the illusion to worth consciousness determines whether you revert to the familiar illusion or you reconnect permanently to the worth you were born with and are here to express. It's the "spiritual buoyancy" Rev. Michael Bernard Beckwith refers to when we're in that space between levels of consciousness.

Thoughts emanating from an illusion of unworthiness are negative in their nature and attract experiences that make the illusion feel real. Complaints, judgment, gossip, pity parties, whining, excuses, comparisons, etc. flow freely from an illusion of unworthiness and people who engage in them feel justified in expressing such rancor. They are unaware of the vicious cycle they're traveling, which begins with their thoughts, attracts the experience, which leads to thoughts about the experience, which brings more matching experiences – and the cycle continues.

People living from an illusion of unworthiness are more likely to think negative thoughts habitually, often without realizing just how negative the thoughts are. When they experience a stressful situation, they are likely to say something like, "if it's not one thing, it's another." Or if they're about to embark on a major project, they'll probably embrace Murphy's Law, "if anything can go wrong, it will," because they are unaware that even seemingly innocuous phrases like these contain negative energy that, according to spiritual law, must attract matching experiences.

Each person is born on purpose with a purpose. Collectively, our primary purpose is to express the divinity within us. Individually, your unique purpose is the gift and talent with your name on it, which is your way of expressing the divine. That thing is not to be denied. Doing so constipates inner splendor, which left unexpressed results in regret. At the end of a person's life, aside from relationship issues, their biggest disappointments center on their unexpressed talent; dreams they never pursued.

Thoughts are essential to the manifestation of our gifts and talents, which will not be silenced. Their job is to get our attention and be made manifest. An illusion of unworthiness will either stop you from delivering your gifts and talents or shape how they manifest. If they are delivered from the illusion of unworthiness, how they show up will be in alignment with the illusion.

The self-doubt and fear that flow from the illusion will either derail the manifestation of the gift and talent or manifest it at a low level that feels like a failure. When the illusion produces an unsuccessful outcome, our self-talk is full of "see, I knew it wouldn't work."

That illusion-fueled manifestation then becomes a memory deposited in our subconscious that pops up whenever we get serious about pursing a goal. The memory reminds us of our past failures to prevent us from trying again. And because the illusion of unworthiness is at the core, we buy into it and unwittingly allow those memories to keep us in our comfort zone; the safe space where risks are unwelcome.

Living from worth consciousness empowers us to think differently about our past. What the illusion of unworthiness brands a failure, worth consciousness sees as an experience. An unsuccessful outcome is seen as a lesson with wisdom to use for future projects when viewed from worth consciousness.

Worth consciousness transforms us into archeologists whose only relationship with the past is from a strength-based perspective. Worth consciousness does not negate the past; however, instead of allowing it to be the story we use to define us, it simply becomes our history. It happened. There's nothing we can do to change that it happened, but worth consciousness flips the victimhood script to a power script with built-in victimhood repellent.

Living from your worth consciousness shapes the quality of your thoughts because living from worth consciousness is intentional. A person who is aware of their innate worth is also aware that their thoughts are powerful and manifest into experiences, so they are mindful of what they think.

They are mindful of external influences that affect the quality of their thoughts so the books they read, the television shows they watch, the music they listen to, the people with whom they converse, the social media posts they make and follow are primarily positive, productive and progressive.

They feed their mind content that aligns with and celebrates their worth consciousness. Thoughts aligned with worth consciousness are primarily life affirming, positive, healthy and prosperous and they manifest experiences that are primarily life affirming, positive, healthy and prosperous.

WORTHY NOTES:

THE FORGIVENESS FACTOR

As it relates to dissolving the illusion of unworthiness and living from your worth consciousness, forgiveness is a non-negotiable part of the process. And while either forgiving someone who has harmed you or being willing to forgive them is extremely important, on the worthiness reconnection journey, you're encouraged to go even deeper.

Be mindful that forgiveness is a powerful gift to yourself that neither minimizes what happened to you nor implies you condone it. Forgiveness operates on a spectrum of power and there is value in considering forgiveness at all. People who may have progressed from the staunch refusal to forgive stance, to becoming willing to do so have obviously made important progress in alleviating some distress.

But merely being willing to forgive and taking the first steps to forgiveness, while beneficial, do not have the power necessary for dissolving the illusion of unworthiness. Dissolving the illusion is a bold move that can transform your life. It requires embracing and acting on bold ideas that change you at your core.

"If you always do, what you've always done, you'll always get, what you've always got."

Our traditional forgiveness approach contains remnants of victimhood - judging, blaming, accusing, playing the injured party and seeking revenge, and victimhood maintains the illusion of unworthiness because it makes someone else responsible for your peace. It says if someone else did something to harm you, there is something they must change about their behavior or their belief about their behavior before you can experience the peace you're desiring.

People determined to hold on to the anger and resentment from past hurts often feel justified in their refusal to forgive as though remaining angry and resentful is somehow teaching their offender a lesson.

You are worthy. Period. There is no experience that can change that. Piercing the illusion of unworthiness, engaging gratitude surrounding its presence in your life, changing the way you see it immerses you into the energy of your worth consciousness.

From that organically expanding energy comes the power to approach forgiveness from an entirely different perspective that might be challenging to comprehend but liberates from the inside-out.

The approach is called Radical Forgiveness and it is a game changer. Radical Forgiveness and worth consciousness go hand in hand because both deliver you from victim mentality. Victimhood and worth consciousness cannot coexist and the more fully you occupy your worth consciousness, the less appealing victimhood feels.

In his life-changing book, "Radical Forgiveness," the late Colin C. Tipping says, "By reminding us that we are spiritual beings having a human experience, Radical Forgiveness raises our vibration and moves us in the direction of spiritual evolution."

Tipping differentiates between "forgiveness that maintains the victim archetype and Radical Forgiveness that frees us from it. Radical Forgiveness challenges us to radically shift our perception of the world and our interpretations of what happens to us in our lives so we can stop being a victim." Radical forgiveness relinquishes you from the illusion of unworthiness and victimhood because it guides you to look at life's hurts from the elevated vantagepoint of your soul.

His approach is called radical for a reason. It's not for folk interested in the "I can forgive, but I can't forget" mentality. And it's not for people who give lip service to forgiveness but keep the experience alive by constantly revisiting or rehashing.

Our illusion of unworthiness results from us assigning meaning to our life's experiences that become beliefs that are stored in our subconscious. The experience does not determine our worth because nothing can. We are born worthy; however, the subconscious beliefs attract matching experiences that reinforce our illusion of unworthiness.

Radical Forgiveness provides us the means to transform the subconscious belief by recognizing the experiences it continues to attract into our life as opportunities to heal the distorted belief that gave rise to our illusion of unworthiness.

I've used the Radical Forgiveness process over the years with great results, however, the most powerful, freeing Radical Forgiveness experience did not occur until I was 56 years old and was convinced I'd done all the *major* forgiveness work I needed to do.

How timely that during the spring of 2019, I studied forgiveness via A Course in Miracles with Pastor Yolanda Batts in her masterful class, 50 Days to Fearless Living at Celebration Spiritual Center. Several of our assignments were centered on forgiveness, which I completed, but without really recognizing a lingering experience that was subconsciously begging for forgiveness work.

It involves a family friend whose connection to us goes back to before my mother's death. Wanda was extremely close to us, sharing an especially tight friendship with my older brother, Dwayne. I have loving childhood memories of spending time with her and her family, having talent shows, her braiding my hair and other pleasant experiences.

The memory that stands out most vividly, however, is the sunny afternoon when she stood in our backyard with a butcher knife threatening to kill herself. I don't remember why she was suicidal, but I know it had something to do with some turmoil happening with her family and Wanda's desire to move in with us. I remember that my mother, with whom she shared a close relationship, intervened and eventually talked Wanda out of harming herself and returning to her home.

My memories of Wanda's presence in our lives from that point on are sketchy and we did eventually lose contact after Ma's death in 1974. We reconnected years later and Wanda's immersion into our family was quick and deep. She started spending time with us and was a regular guest at gatherings with our extended family.

Many more years would pass before her connection to my paternal relatives in New Jersey would occur and become a catalyst in my Radical Forgiveness work. My brother, Dwayne, moved back to our birth state after our oldest brother, Skip, was murdered in 1989. Long story short, many years later, Wanda called Dwayne after a death in her family and instead of reaching him, she reached my cousin Lisa and the two of them eventually developed a beautiful and close friendship that has lasted for years.

Meanwhile in Miami, Wanda's presence in our lives began to mysteriously grate my nerves. Something about her was unusually annoying and I no longer enjoyed spending time with her. I could not put my finger on why, so I tried to pin it on personality traits and just told myself that not everyone is meant to have a close relationship.

I found it amusing that she and my cousin Lisa continued getting closer, visiting each other and traveling together, but didn't give myself permission to explore whatever feelings I had about their friendship, so I tucked them away.

When Lisa's mother, my Aunt Ruth, transitioned from Alzheimer's Disease in 2017, an experience on the day of her funeral began to give shape to my issues with Wanda. Aunt Ruth was known for her extensive church hat collection, so my cousin Carla suggested that Aunt Ruth's two daughters and her nieces honor our beloved aunt by each wearing one of her hats to the funeral. The first cousins agreed it was an excellent idea and excitedly modeled hats the night before the funeral, helping each other choose the most flattering one while we reminisced about Aunt Ruth and her presence in our lives.

On the morning of the funeral, we all met at Aunt Ruth's house and as we prepared to leave for the church, Wanda walks into the living room wearing one of my aunt's hats, the only non-cousin to sport one. Seeing her wearing the hat pissed me off. I pushed the angst that rose in my chest back down, breathed deeply, swallowed hard and tried to conceal my disappointment. It took me a few minutes to get myself together and I did so by intentionally thinking about my loving, generous aunt and how she would have zero problems with Wanda wearing the hat along with her daughters and nieces. After scanning the room for others' responses and finding none, I determined I must be the only one with a problem, so I let it go.

Later that year, I confessed my displeasure about what I felt was Wanda's insensitive invasion into our special remembrance of Aunt Ruth to Lisa during a drive from Atlantic City to Newark. Fast forward to the summer of 2019 during another drive, this time from Newark to Baltimore and Lisa asks me why I don't like Wanda. I explain that although I love her, there's just something I can't put my finger on. I chalked it up to our personalities just not meshing. Lisa said she didn't understand why I felt that way, especially since our relationship goes back so far.

For weeks, I could not shake the conversation with Lisa and became preoccupied with it. It didn't seem to be such a big deal, but it nagged me at night before I went to bed and would pop up unexpectedly throughout the day. When Wanda visited Lisa in New Jersey a couple of weeks later, several of us went out to what was a pleasant dinner that felt only slightly awkward because I assumed Lisa was wondering about my feelings towards Wanda. I also wondered whether she'd shared her thoughts with Wanda.

Exhausted, I fell asleep quickly when I get home but woke up the next morning feeling deep dread about Wanda. I wondered, what the heck is going on? I didn't want to take the convoluted energy into my morning prayer and meditation, so I decided to complete a Radical Forgiveness worksheet to resolve the issue once and for all so I could move on.

I did not expect what happened next. Completing the Radical Forgiveness process regarding Wanda was undoubtedly the most emotional, most freeing and totally transformative experience I've ever had. The process includes a series of questions to help you get clear about the real reason you're aggravated with the person, because we are never upset for the reason we think we are!

The process unearthed a visit I made from Miami to New Jersey in 1990, a year after Skip's murder and Dwayne's relocation to the Garden State. I had been really looking forward to this visit, and leading up to it, I'd anticipated reconnecting to my paternal family, my daddy's two sisters, Aunt Ruth and Aunt Catherine, as well as all my first cousins. I had not visited New Jersey since attending my father's funeral in 1988.

While completing the Radical Forgiveness process, I could recall the excitement I'd felt about the visit and how I expected everyone to be thrilled to see me. They were not. And once I arrived, who I would stay with during my visit also became an issue. I spent the night at two different relatives' homes before my cousin Peggy stepped in and allowed me to spend the rest of my trip at her townhouse.

Embarrassed and hurt, I returned to Miami disillusioned about my relationship with my family. I spoke of it to no one. Lisa and I would have a passive aggressive argument via greeting cards several years later, but other than that, any resentment, anger or pain remained unacknowledged, tucked away, unexpressed and largely unrecognized. That is until I completed the Radical Forgiveness form about Wanda.

It helped me to zero in on the underlying belief that had been stirring around inside me and the reason I had unconsciously begun to find her so annoying - the woman had stolen my family. They'd welcomed her with open arms and loved on her unconditionally after treating me like an intruder when I visited in 1990. Pain I didn't even realize existed rose to the surface and had me sobbing during that aspect of the Radical Forgiveness experience.

The process is comprehensive and involves writing out your personal victimized perspective, especially how it made you feel, so I described Wanda's "theft" of my family and how rejected, abandoned, and disregarded I felt. I wrote down how they preferred her to me and how she liked to boast about how much "her" family loves her. I really got into it and feelings that I'd apparently repressed came rushing to the surface.

Here's the kicker, Radical Forgiveness is so comprehensive in its healing that it ultimately helps you realize that whatever expectations, disappointment, etc. you're feeling about the other person are really feelings you have about yourself; feelings you're projecting onto them. The forgiving experience compels you to examine yourself; an imperative part of the process. Being willing to look at who you were, who you are and unveiling who you want to be is a part of the healing that comes with Radical Forgiveness.

The process helped me see how I'd learned to guard myself because of all the losses and the sexual abuse; guardedness that spilled over to the way I protected my emotional self. I had a difficult time trusting people so I always kept a safe distance and would let no one get too close. Interestingly, I craved love, felt entitled to it and expected my family to demonstrate their love for me even though I wasn't demonstrating it to them.

Radical Forgiveness is deeply spiritual, and when done thoroughly, will include Source guiding you to your healing. I must have been ready for this healing because during the two hours I was immersed in Radical Forgiveness, I came to appreciate that Wanda is pure love. Deep admiration for her unapologetic approach to receiving the love she knew she deserved flowed along with the buckets of tears. She has a no-holds barred approach to embracing the love she felt was missing in her own family. She hit the jackpot with mine.

As I was completing the Radical Forgiveness process early that Friday morning, I could feel the transformation happening within me. All the emotions that I'd repressed about my family, Wanda and the dynamics that fueled the previous resentment towards her came to the surface and lifted away so completely it literally felt like a boulder was removed from my shoulders.

In an instant, I could see Wanda in an entirely different way. It filled me with overwhelming admiration for her diligence and then intensely emotional gratitude that she experiences true, bona fide, soul stirring love from some amazing people; people she connected with because she's an amazing woman.

I was sobbing again, but this time with the most loving vibrations flowing through me. In that moment, I could see how every single thing had to happen the way it did. I had to connect with Wanda when I was a little girl. She had to have the experiences she had with her own family. She had to connect with my family. My family had to love her deeply and I had to have that jacked up visit, feel sorry for myself and begin to resent Wanda.

Wanda had to remain present in my life, aggravate me by rocking Aunt Ruth's hat, and Lisa had to question my feelings so that the discomfort would push me to the Radical Forgiveness process that helped me experience the most gratifying forgiveness ever. Interestingly, when I began the process, I thought I was forgiving Wanda for something, but in typical Radical Forgiveness style, I ended up forgiving myself and being totally grateful for Wanda.

I owned the underlying jealousy I felt about her relationship with Lisa and not only did it instantly disappear, it was replaced with genuine appreciation that my family's love provides Wanda with what she needs, what she deserves.

Everyone had a role to play and guided by our souls, we provided each other with exactly what we needed. I could see the big picture and I liked what I saw. Tipping said in his book that when we can recognize the blessing in an experience that previously produced pain, its trajectory, from origin to culmination, might not make sense to anyone except the person experiencing the freedom it manifested.

I know from firsthand experience that Radical Forgiveness is a powerful, life-changing process that is essential to living from worth consciousness. I didn't even realize how much of my energy was being consumed and now that I've done the work, there's nothing blocking the energy of my worth from flowing freely.

Our relationships provide ideal opportunities to practice Radical Forgiveness. Another example of how powerful the process is involves the author's sister's marriage and its near demise. Tipping's sister, Jill, was in distress (living from an illusion of unworthiness) because of family dynamics involving her husband and his daughter from a previous relationship.

The daughter's husband had been killed in a car accident and as a result, Jill's husband began to spend significantly more time with her. Apparently, Jill was feeling neglected by her husband because of what she felt was the obsessive affection he showered on his daughter; affection he did not show her.

Prior to witnessing it displayed towards her stepdaughter, Jill believed her husband was incapable of demonstrating affection. She felt that her husband's behavior changed swiftly and included strange aspects that had begun to claw at their relationship. He didn't understand why she was upset, thought she was the one behaving weirdly and blamed her for the unraveling of their marriage. Jill was at her wit's end and nearly ready to divorce him.

When she visited Tipping, he helped her to see how dynamics between her and their father when she was a little girl were at the root of her marital issues. Their father was a rather unaffectionate man, or so Jill thought because of his distance and lack of affection towards her. The initial meaning Jill assigned to her father's lack of affection was she was not enough and was unworthy of her father's love. When she was a little older, she worked through her disappointment and arrived at the conclusion that her dad was simply incapable of showing affection. Figuring that's just the way he is, she felt some relief that she was not the cause of his distant behavior.

Her insecurities were triggered when she saw her father doting on her little niece (Colin Tipping's daughter). Jill's theory about his inability to show affection was shattered and, even though she was in her 20s, Jill became convinced he just did not love her. The meaning she assigned to the experience was she was not enough, and she would never be enough for any man to love her – an illusion of unworthiness that attracted men into her life whose behavior reinforced her belief.

Tipping helped her to look at their father's behavior objectively. He did not hug her. He did not sit her on his lap and talk to her. As children do, she personalized and blamed herself for her dad's lack of affection. Jill also repressed the experience to minimize its pain. She tucked it away and went on to live a relatively happy life, but because she never resolved it, she created an illusion of unworthiness that attracted adult relationships that triggered her rejection issues.

Tipping helped her understand how the situation with her husband and his daughter presented her an opportunity to heal her past daddy/daughter issues because it was rooted in the distorted belief she created and internalized as a little girl. Unhealed childhood hurts often get repressed and when triggered in adulthood, can cause regression and emotions that seem to make no sense.

The Radical Forgiveness approach explains that our souls attract opportunity after opportunity for us to heal from hurts (mostly rooted in childhood) through our adult relationships. It explains why although we leave one unhealthy relationship, we can end up with a different person with the same issues.

The repressed, unhealed emotional angst stemming from the meaning we assigned a childhood experience will continue to attract mirroring relationships until we heal the hurt. Tipping helped his sister heal her childhood hurt by helping her consider, perhaps their father showed his love in other ways, like staying up all night to build a dollhouse Jill cherished. And even though someone might not express their love demonstrably does not mean they do not love you. Further, basing your worth on how someone feels about you saps your power. No one defines your worth. Not even a parent.

One of my experiences with radical forgiveness, like Jill's, involved my father. Initially learning more about the generous, kind, funny man he was felt counterproductive. How come I was not the recipient of his generosity, kindness and humor, I reasoned. But radical forgiveness helped me see the bigger picture and consider that inner turmoil prevented him from giving to me what he couldn't give to himself. If my daddy could have done better, he would have. Further, regardless of what his capabilities were, my father was not responsible for my happiness; a realization that freed me from looking to anyone else for my joy and was instrumental in me reclaiming my power.

When we can make the connection and radically forgive, resentment for the person with whom we have the issue can turn to gratitude for presenting us the opportunity to heal. From that space of healing, the distorted subconscious belief can be replaced with a new belief that flows from our worth consciousness and attracts experiences that match its affirming energy.

Radical Forgiveness is a portal to worth consciousness. You can access the free Radical Forgiveness forms and Tipping's amazing book at MichelleHollinger.com.

WORTHY NOTES:

Are You Worthy?

CELEBRATE

Are You Worthy?

LETTER TO
YOUR YOUNGER SELF

It's important to consider that every experience that created the illusion of unworthiness has already happened. It's a part of your past and the reason our past continually trips us up is because we primarily focus on it from a deficit perspective. Instead of allowing your past to run your life, you can recreate your relationship to it through Radical Forgiveness and strength-based retrospection.

Ignoring the past is out of the question because as Dr. Joe Dispenza explains, thinking is the language of the mind and feelings are the language of the body. The energy from past emotions is stored in our body, which acts as our unconscious mind, and gets triggered by certain experiences. It explains why past events that generated the deepest emotions are the events we remember most vividly. It also explains why Maya Angelou's quote, "I've learned that people will forget what you said, people will forget what you did, but people will never forget how you made them feel," is so powerfully true.

Dr. Joe's body of work, including his books, "You Are the Placebo," and "Becoming Supernatural," is an outstanding approach to detaching from the emotions of the past and learning to use your worth consciousness to create your future.

As it relates to reconnecting to your worth consciousness, your past plays a key role. Since past experiences and the meanings assigned to them can lead to the development of an illusion of unworthiness, examining and revising the meanings is a powerful approach to changing your relationship with your past. If you only revisit your past to bemoan it or to tell your younger self what you could have done differently, you give it power and remain its hostage.

To shift the power dynamic, try this very effective strength-based approach to redefining your past. Write a letter to your younger self, but from an entirely different perspective than you've likely seen in magazines or on TV shows. The typical intention behind this type of letter can feel productive. Now that you're older and wiser, giving advice to your younger self can feel like a pleasant gesture that somehow helps your younger self be better.

If you're already living from your worth consciousness, while giving advice to your younger self serves no real purpose, it's probably harmless. It you're still dealing with the illusion of unworthiness, however, offering your younger self advice about how you could have done things differently or been a better person reinforces the illusion.

Sitting from this vantage point, Monday morning quarterbacking our past allows us to see what we could've done differently; how we could have been more - if only we knew then, what we know now. But that's impossible.

It's a deficit-focused approach that implies you *could* have done things differently when you couldn't have. It's an unfair approach because at this vantage point, years later, you have amassed more wisdom, courage and insight, so of course your assessment of past behavior is different.

Although you can clearly see now that your 25-year old self could have exercised more courage or confidence, your 25-year old self was operating from an entirely different consciousness and had no way of knowing. He/she really was doing the best he/she could, with what they had.

Plus, "coulda, woulda, shoulda" advice reinforces the illusion of unworthiness because it is essentially telling your younger self, "you were not enough."

The letter I'm asking you to write doesn't criticize, minimize or offer advice to your younger self because - what's the point? You cannot change one thing about your past or your younger self and offering hollow advice does nothing to dissolve the illusion.

The letter I'm encouraging you to write is a strength-based letter that celebrates your worth. Its intention is for you to change the way you look at this aspect of your past so that what you see changes. To that end, the letter that you write to your younger self is a letter of gratitude that celebrates who you were and what you accomplished, instead of focusing on who you were not and what you didn't do or didn't do well.

Make it a special, sacred occasion. Find a quiet space and carve out some solo time. Get some nice stationary and a favorite pen. Light a candle. Be fully present.

Think about what your younger self achieved and thank her or him for it. Think about what he or she endured and thank him or her for it. Think about what she survived and thank her for it. Think about his talents, gifts and skills and thank him for them. Think about the personality trait others didn't understand but you grew into and thank your younger self for holding on to it. Think about how her navigation of her life's circumstances made it possible for you to be here, now, and thank her for it. Think of all the wonderful qualities your younger self had and whether they were noticed or not, thank him for them. Be sure to tell him or her just how worthy they have always been.

There is no page limit to this love letter. And you don't have to finish it in one sitting. Add to it over the next few days, weeks, months. Continue to add to it for as long as you like. And while you're at it, consider how the qualities you're thanking your younger self for exist within your worth consciousness and are still present within you – NOW.

How can you put them to use?

WORTHY NOTES:

I AM WORTHY
GRATITUDE JOURNAL

Worth consciousness and gratitude are mutually connected; they naturally reinforce each other. Gratitude plays an essential role in dissolving your illusion of unworthiness because it flows from your worth. It activates the Law of Attraction, which says focusing on what you're grateful for manifests more things for which to be grateful.

But the law works both ways. Although you have numerous experiences occurring in your life every day that remind you of your worth, they often go unnoticed because the human tendency is to focus on experiences that flow from and reinforce the illusion.

When you're living from the illusion, you are far more likely to obsess over what went wrong and complain about what you don't have, unwittingly attracting negative experiences and circumstances of lack.

What you focus on takes intention. It is a choice. Choosing to live from gratitude by focusing on experiences that remind you of your worth expands your worth consciousness.

Gratitude is a game changer and writing is creative. Combining them both in an #IAMWORTHY gratitude journal is an intentionally powerful way to celebrate your worth. When you notice the wonderful things about you and put them in writing, you become even more mindful of how worthy you are. Capturing experiences that remind you of your worth manifests more worth-reminding experiences.

Here's how it works: purchase a beautiful journal and each day, write at least three things that remind you that you're worthy. Tell no one about your journal and make it for your eyes only. On those challenging days where writing about experiences that celebrate your worth might be a struggle, look through some of your previous entries as a reminder.

There are no rules to follow because worthiness is subjective. You know what makes you feel worthy. Write it down and magnify its power in your life.

WORTHY NOTES:

SELF-VALIDATION
VISION BOARD

Take an amazing selfie.

What you do with it next might be difficult, but it's powerful. Do not, I repeat, do not post it on social media. At all. I know the urge to share it with others in anticipation of all the likes, loves and comments about how great you look is so very tempting. But as it relates to worth consciousness, the external validation that comes from social media is counterproductive.

Self-validation is far more important, so instead of sharing your awesome selfie with others, you're going to keep it all for yourself and use it as a beautiful reminder of who you are, to strengthen great qualities you're already using and to cultivate other wonderful qualities you want to express.

Here's what you do with your selfie:

Look at it. Really look at it and notice what you love about the person in it. Start with your appearance. What's your favorite part of your face? What do you like most about this selfie? Look into your eyes.

Now, write a mini-bio. Where were you born, when? Where did you attend elementary school, middle/junior high, high school? Did you attend college? Vocational school? If so, where?

Make a list of your strengths.

Recall an accomplishment that you felt great about. Re-live it. What was it? When did it happen? How did you feel? Which qualities were necessary to make it happen?

Write them down.

Next, print your selfie and place it in the center of a poster board. Now go back to the strengths and qualities you identified about yourself. Either type them up and print them out individually; or find large versions of the words in magazines or newspapers and cut them out.

The qualities you already use, place them closely around your selfie and glue them to the poster board. Now around those words, glue the qualities that you want to begin expressing.

The final step of creating your Self-Validation Vision Board™ is to cut out images, photos, etc. that represent the most important goals you have for yourself. If it's traveling, cut out an image of a plane, train or whichever mode of transportation you plan to use to get there. Cut out an image of the destination you plan to visit.

Starting a small business? Cut out an image that represents the type of business you'll be starting. What is the name of your business? Type out the name, print it and glue it to your board. Add other images that represent your dreams and goals to the outer areas of your poster board.

The idea for this powerful visual image is to reinforce awesome qualities you already use and set an intention to cultivate the additional qualities you want to express. Ultimately, the purpose of your vision board is to celebrate your worth by combining a visual image of your amazing qualities with the power of visualization to manifest your dreams and goals.

The foundation for living your best life is worth consciousness and your Self-Validation Vision Board™ is a powerful tool to help manifest it.

WORTHY NOTES:

_____

_____

_____

_____

_____

_____

_____

_____

_____

_____

_____

_____

_____

_____

_____

_____

_____

_____

_____

_____

_____

_____

Are You Worthy?

THE WORTHY MEDITATION

Engaging with and expanding your worth consciousness is a spiritual process that requires spending time in the silence. Because your innate worth rests inside of you, going within is the only way to reconnect with this sacred, totally amazing part of your inner being.

Shutting off the external noise, for at least a few minutes each day, is essential to familiarizing yourself with your worth consciousness and ultimately facilitating its expansion. It sits there waiting and will respond to the attention you place upon it while in the silence.

I refer to 'the silence,' instead of mere silence because there is a big difference. Silence is simply the absence of noise. 'The Silence' is sacred and full of spiritual wisdom ready to reveal itself when you close the door to the outside world and seek what it has to offer.

Begin with five minutes. For the next twenty-one days, sit quietly in a comfortable setting where you will not be disturbed. Breathe slowly and deeply with your eyes closed. Allow the inevitable thoughts about picking up your dry cleaning and what you will cook for dinner to float on by.

When an errant thought appears, continue bringing your attention back to your breathing. For the first two minutes, inhale deeply – in through your nose and exhale by making the sound ahhhh through your mouth. For the remaining three minutes, while continuing to breathe slowly and deeply, repeat silently in your mind, over and over and over, "I am worthy."

Complete your meditation with a few more deep breaths, slowly open your eyes and congratulate yourself for taking this special time for yourself. At the end of the twenty-one days, add to your spiritual practice by reading a book or some written material that reminds you of your worth. Continuing to meditate is a powerful way to celebrate and nurture your worth.

Spending between five and fifteen minutes each day, preferably in the morning, is a wonderful way to energize your worth consciousness before starting your day.

If you're new to meditation and would prefer trying a guided experience, check out The Worthy Meditation, a free 8-minute guided meditation by visiting my website, https://MichelleHollinger.com.

WORTHY NOTES:

BONDAGE (ILLUSION OF UNWORTHINESS) OR LIBERTY (WORTH CONSCIOUSNESS) WHICH?

In addition to the Bible, the foundational book for Unity and many other New Thought spiritual centers is *Lessons in Truth* (first printing, 1903; fifty first printing, 1999) by H. Emilie Cade, a homeopathic physician who treated her patients both medically and spiritually.

It provides an excellent road map to understanding New Thought philosophy and presents spiritual concepts that "show us how to increase our personal empowerment and enhance our spiritual growth."

The title of the first chapter, Bondage or Liberty, Which? makes it clear that how we travel this journey called our life is up to us. The book teaches that the primary cause of human suffering is forgetfulness. We forget our divinity. We forget how powerful we really are. We forget that we're worthy.

Bondage (illusion of unworthiness) or Liberty (worth consciousness), which? We get to choose whether we experience life in bondage; existing as a spectator, living by default, responding to whatever shows up and hanging out in our comfort zone because it feels safe. Choosing this option involves mediocrity, victimhood, playing small and conforming to external expectations for how we live.

Living from an illusion of unworthiness is living in bondage. The illusion cleverly disguises divine discontent so that it feels like stress, which most people believe is a normal part of their life and therefore expect to experience, indefinitely. At high, anxiety producing levels, stress can lead to illness, but instead of exploring its root cause - people are prescribed medication – often with side-effects worse than the original diagnosis. Treating the illnesses that result from unworthiness externally does nothing to dissolve the unworthiness. The medication might remedy the symptoms, but the illusion remains a part of your consciousness and can continue to manifest stress-related illness, frustration, mediocrity and other telltale signs of unworthiness.

Living from worth consciousness liberates you to live your best life in every aspect of it; health, wealth, relationships, career and spirituality. Worth consciousness reveals your purpose; and each person is here on purpose, with a purpose. Collectively, our purpose is to express our divinity. Individually, you are here to express the gifts and talents **with your name on them.**

Encased within your worth consciousness is everything you need to live the life you were born to live, which includes expressing your unique purpose and enjoying being you. Becoming familiar with the energy flowing from your worth consciousness takes courage, but you get to decide.

Illusion of unworthiness or worth consciousness? Which?

Bondage (Illusion of Unworthiness) or Liberty (Worth Consciousness) Which?

WORTHY NOTES:

_____

_____

_____

_____

_____

_____

_____

_____

_____

_____

_____

_____

_____

_____

_____

_____

_____

_____

WORTHY RESOURCES

BOOKS

Key to Yourself
Venice Bloodworth

The Universe is Calling
Eric Butterworth

Lessons in Truth
H. Emilie Cade

Becoming Supernatural
Dr. Joe Dispenza

You Are the Placebo
Dr. Joe Dispenza

You Can Heal Your Life
Louise Hay

Radical Forgiveness
Colin C. Tipping

A Return to Love
Marianne Williamson

ONLINE MATERIAL

Dr. Joe Dispenza
www.drjoedispenza.com

Rev. Ike Legacy, LLC
www.RevIke.org

Eckart Tolle
www.eckharttolle.com

Iyanla Vanzant
www.Iyanla.co

Gary Zukav
www.seatofthesoul.com

SPIRITUAL CENTERS

Agape International
www.agapelive.com

Celebration Spiritual Center
www.celebrationsc.org

Universal Foundation for Better Living
www.ufbl.org

Unity Worldwide Ministries
www.unityworldwideministries.org

ABOUT THE AUTHOR

Michelle Hollinger is a metaphysical New Thought student. Michelle is the founder and publisher of *The Sisterhood*, a magazine for women; author of The Sisterhood Exchange as well as a filmmaker. The former editor of *The Miami Times* and the *South Florida Times*, she is also a sociologist and a former social worker. She's the author of two books for the child welfare industry, *The ABCs of Authentic Worth with Families* and *Seven Steps to Strengthen Your Family*.

She earned the Master Certificate from the Johnnie Colemon Theological Seminary and was a prayer chaplain at Unity on the Bay and the Universal Truth Center, both located in Miami.

Michelle lives in New Jersey, is the mother of three awesome children; Alexandra, Stephanie and Tyler; and the grandma of the amazing Naomi Michelle.

EPILOGUE

Since beginning my journey to reconnect with my worth, my life has changed tremendously. I didn't realize it at the time, but the journey began when I filed for divorce after 26 years of marriage; which was built on the illusion of unworthiness with hefty doses of narcissism and people-pleasing.

After numerous attempts for a collective embrace of our worth, it became necessary for me to focus exclusively on my individual journey.

I have since moved from Florida to New Jersey and one of the biggest benefits to living from my worth consciousness has been releasing over 50 pounds from my body.

My spiritual journey continues with guidance from two spiritual geniuses, Walden Award honorees Pastor Greg Stamper and Pastor Yolanda Batts, co-founders of Celebration Spiritual Center in Brooklyn. PG and PY, as they're affectionately known, are big on worthiness. To experience their brilliant perspective on your innate worth, check out the sermon series, The Worthy Project, on YouTube at https://youtu.be/1IOGlCtEPfU.

Made in the USA
Las Vegas, NV
16 September 2021